D0645435

TCU

DAILY DEVOTIONS FOR DIE-HARD FANS

HORNED FROGS

Daily Devotions for Die-Hard Fans: TCU Horned Frogs
© 2013 Ed McMinn
Extra Point Publishers; P.O. Box 871; Perry, GA 31069

All rights reserved, including the right to reproduce this book or portions thereof in any form whatsoever.

Library of Congress Cataloging-in-Publication Data
13 ISBN Digit ISBN: 978-0-9882595-3-9

Manufactured in the United States of America.

Unless otherwise noted, scripture quotations are taken from the *Holy Bible, New International Version*. Copyright © 1973, 1978, 1984, by the International Bible Society. All rights reserved.

Visit us at www.die-hardfans.com.

Cover and interior design by John Powell
Some research by Jordan Welsh

Every effort has been made to identify copyright holders. Any omissions are unintentional. Extra Point Publishers should be notified in writing immediately for full acknowledgement in future editions.

HORNED FROGS

Dedicated
To the Greater Glory
of God

The following titles are available:

IN THE BEGINNING

Read Genesis 1, 2:1-3.

"God saw all that he had made, and it was very good" (v. 1:31).

The school wasn't named Texas Christian University, they weren't the Horned Frogs, and they weren't even in Fort Worth. Nevertheless, in 1896, a group of students led by a pair of professors began what became TCU football.

In 1873 in Thorp Spring, Texas, brothers Addison and Randolph Clark founded AddRan Male & Female College, the first coed institution of higher learning west of the Mississippi River. The school moved to Waco in 1895.

Late in the fall of 1896, some students decided to form a football team and take on another Waco school. They didn't have a coach, but professors Addison Clark, Jr., and A.C. Easley stepped up to provide some leadership.

They challenged their counterparts at Toby Business School to a game. On Dec. 7, the two teams met on the AddRan campus in a game that bore little resemblance to college football as we know it today.

Halfback Claude McClellan crossed the goal line in the first half to score the first touchdown in school history. An AddRan player named Burger, his first name apparently lost to history, turned in the play of the day when he broke loose for a 50-yard touchdown run in the second half. That turned out to be the game winner as AddRan won 8-6.

The school newspaper, *The AddRan Collegian*, bragged that "our boys fought the game without calling on the substitutes." The publication looked ahead to more games, regarding the win over Toby "as good practice for the battle with the Houston Heavyweights team." That first football team played the Heavyweights twice, losing 22-0 before forging a 0-0 tie.

1897 saw the hiring of the first coach, Joe J. Field, and the arrival of the Horned Frogs as the mascot. The school was renamed TCU in 1902, but this was years after football had officially begun.

Beginnings are important, but what we make of them is even more important. Consider, for example, how far the TCU football program has come since that first season. Every morning, you get a gift from God: a new beginning. God hands to you as an expression of divine love a new day full of promise and the chance to right the wrongs in your life. You can use the day to pay a debt, start a new relationship, replace a burned-out light bulb, tell your family you love them, chase a dream, solve a nagging problem . . . or not.

God simply provides the gift. How you use it is up to you. People often talk wistfully about starting over or making a new beginning. God gives you the chance with the dawning of every new day. You have the chance today to make things right – and that includes your relationship with God.

The AddRan boys were too strong for Toby's team.
-- The AddRan Collegian on the first-ever TCU football game

**Every day is not just a dawn; it is a
precious chance to start over or begin anew.**

DAY 2

REDEEMED

Read 1 Peter 1:17-25.

"It was not with perishable things such as silver or gold that you were redeemed from the empty way of life handed down to you from your forefathers, but with the precious blood of Christ" (vv. 18-19).

Andy Dalton found his redemption on one of the biggest stages in sports: the Rose Bowl.

From 2007-2010, Dalton put together a career that left him as the holder of every major TCU quarterback record. In 2009 and in 2010, he was the Mountain West Conference Offensive Player of the Year. He had a 42-7 record as a starting quarterback, shattering the previous school record of 29 set by Sammy Baugh (1934-36). In 2010, he finished ninth in the voting for the Heisman Trophy.

But in the biggest game in the history of modern TCU football to that point -- the 2010 Fiesta Bowl -- Dalton had what one ESPN writer called the worst game of his career. He was intercepted three times and the Frogs were upset by Boise State 17-10.

Dalton took much of the blame for the loss on his shoulders, and the disappointment was "something I didn't want to feel again," he said. So when the matchup for the 2011 Rose Bowl was announced -- TCU vs. Wisconsin -- he realized he had a chance for redemption. After all, this game would eclipse the bowl game of the previous season in its magnitude.

He went to work. He quit cracking jokes and laughing in the

locker room. He studied films to the point that he said of the Badger defense, "I knew everything they were doing."

Dalton delivered in a big way. He completed 15 of 23 passes for 219 yards and a touchdown and led TCU in rushing while notching a second TD on the ground. He was the game's offensive MVP, leading the Frogs to a 21-19 win that capped a 13-0 season.

He was also "the guy who led this team this far, and it was his job to finish it off," said tailback Ed Wesley. In the process, Dalton found his redemption.

In our capitalistic society, we know all about redemption. Just think "rebate" or store or product coupons. To receive the rebates or the discount, though, we must redeem them, cash them in.

"Redemption" is a business term; it reconciles a debt, restoring one party to favor by making amends, as was the case with Andy Dalton. In the Bible, a slave could obtain his freedom only when a redeemer paid money. In other words, redemption involves the cancelling of a debt the individual cannot pay on his own.

While literal, physical slavery is incomprehensible to us today, we nevertheless live much like slaves in our relationship to sin. On our own, we cannot escape from its consequence, which is death. We need a redeemer, someone to pay the debt that gives us the forgiveness from sin we cannot give ourselves.

We have such a redeemer. He is Jesus Christ, who paid our debt not with money, but with his own blood.

I was really focused because I knew I wanted to play well in this game.
-- Andy Dalton on seeking redemption in the Rose Bowl

To accept Jesus Christ as your savior is to believe
that his death was a selfless act of redemption.

THE GREATEST

Read Mark 9:33-37.

"If anyone wants to be first, he must be the very last, and the servant of all" (v. 35).

It has gone down in Horned Frog lore as the greatest at-bat in TCU baseball history and among the greatest in the history of the College World Series.

Coach Jim Schlossnagle's 2010 Horned Frogs won the school's fifth straight Mountain West Conference championship and set a school record with 54 wins. Most importantly, they made it to the College World Series for the first time in the program's history.

In Omaha, they drubbed FSU 8-1 before losing to UCLA; that defeat set up an elimination game against the Seminoles. As the Frogs batted in the top of the eighth, they trailed 7-3.

The inning started slowly enough when third baseman Jantzen Witte reached on one of five FSU errors in the game. Shortstop Taylor Featherston singled, and Witte later scored on an infield out. With two outs, second baseman Jerome Pena walked in front of a double from senior catcher Bryan Holaday, a second-team All-America. That made it a 7-5 game. Sophomore outfielder Jason Coats then walked on a 3-2 pitch.

With the bases loaded and two outs, senior first baseman Matt Curry worked his way to a full count. He then blasted a slider to dead center field. He "immediately turned to the first-base TCU dugout and held both arms out to his teammates -- as he knew he just hit the biggest home run of his life."

Maybe not. When Curry turned to watch the ball, to his horror he saw the FSU center fielder standing at the fence prepared to make a catch. "Schlossnagle said he wanted to drop to his knees and cry when he saw [the FSU player] circling." But the outfielder had merely lost the ball in the lights. Matt Curry had blasted a grand slam described as "one of the greatest moments in the history of [the college world series]." The homer propelled the Frogs into the lead in a game they won 11-7.

We all want to be the greatest. The goal for the Horned Frogs and their fans every season is at least a conference championship. The competition at work is to be the most productive sales person on the staff or the Teacher of the Year. In other words, we define being the greatest in terms of the struggle for personal success. It's nothing new; Jesus' disciples saw greatness in the same way.

As Jesus illustrated, though, greatness in the Kingdom of God has nothing to do with the secular world's understanding of success. Rather, the greatest are those who channel their ambition toward the furtherance of Christ's kingdom through love and service, rather than their own advancement, which is a complete reversal of status and values as the world sees them.

After all, who could be greater than the person who has Jesus for a brother and God for a father? And that's every one of us.

Perhaps the greatest comeback in the TCU program's history.
-- College Baseball 360 *on TCU's win over FSU*

To be great for God has nothing to do with personal advancement and everything to do with the advancement of Christ's kingdom.

A DOG'S LIFE

Read Genesis 6:11-22; 8:1-4.

"God remembered Noah and all the wild animals and the livestock that were with him in the ark" (v. 8:1).

To get to Sonny Gibbs, you had to get past his dog. That went for both his fiancee and the TCU head coach.

Gibbs was a quarterback before his time. He stood 6'7" tall and weighed 230 pounds. He had a 37-inch sleeve and wore a size 74 hat and size 13 football shoes. Such size in a quarterback isn't that unusual in today's college game, but Gibbs played for TCU from 1960-62.

Gibbs was quite comfortable with his big body. "I'd rather be tall than a squatty body," he once said. He used it to earn All-Southwest Conference honors in 1962, be drafted by the Dallas Cowboys, and be inducted into the TCU Lettermen's Hall of Fame.

Gibbs was a country boy who flunked out of TCU his freshman year after his studies began to interfere with his hunting trips and his weekend visits home to Graham. There lived his family, which included his dog, Pepper. Especially Pepper.

Pepper was described, somewhat vaguely, as a "police dog" of some sort, whose picture could always be found in Gibbs' wallet. Unlike, at least in 1962, a photograph of the 5-foot-5 inch blonde whom he married after his senior season at TCU.

Gibbs was so unconcerned about the fame his football abilities brought him that when TCU head coach Abe Martin showed up at the house to sign him to a scholarship, he was playing tennis. "I was walking home when this kid challenged me to a match," Gibbs said. "I took off my shoes and we went at it and I plum [*sic*] forgot the signing." That left Martin face to face with all 100 pounds of Pepper, who wouldn't let him on the porch. "Pepper really scared 'em," Gibbs said with a chortle.

Do you have a dog or two around the place? How about a cat that passes time staring longingly at your caged canary? Kids have gerbils? Maybe you've gone more exotic with a tarantula.

We Americans love our pets; in fact, more households in this country have pets than have children. We not only share our living space with animals we love and protect but also with some – such as roaches and rats – that we seek to exterminate.

None of us, though, has ever had to face anything remotely like what Noah did when he packed God's menagerie into one boat. God expressly determined the dimensions of the ark so it could accommodate his creatures. He thus saved all his varmints from extinction, including the fish, the frogs, and the ducks, who must have been quite delighted with the whole flood business.

The lesson is clear for we who strive to live as God would have us: All living things are under God's care. God doesn't call us to care for and respect just our beloved pets; we are to serve God as stewards of all of his creatures.

She wouldn't hurt anyone. Of course, at night if she didn't know you she might chew on you a little bit.
-- Sonny Gibbs on Pepper

God cares about all his creatures,
and he expects us to respect them too.

DAZED & CONFUSED

Read Genesis 11:1-9.

"There the Lord confused the language of the whole world" (v. 9a).

Harried and hurried, the Frogs got so confused they lined up for a play different from the one the quarterback expected. They scored, of course, and then won the game with a 2-point conversion on a busted play.

Against Arkansas on Oct. 6, 1984, Jim Wacker's Horned Frogs scored two touchdowns and a 2-point conversion in the last ten minutes to win in Fayetteville 32-31. TCU got the ball at its own 20 trailing 31-17 with 10:19 to play and marched 80 yards for a touchdown. QB Anthony Gulley hit running back Kenneth Davis, the conference's Player of the Year and an All-America, with an 18-yard touchdown pass with 7:58 on the clock. 31-24.

After the kickoff, safety Byron Linwood stopped the Hog back at the TCU 12, and Arkansas missed a chip shot field goal. TCU had one last shot, though winning meant traveling 80 yards in 3:45 or less. Again, the Frogs frantically moved down the field. A leaping catch by wide receiver James Maness and a penalty set TCU up at the Hog 2 with 47 seconds left.

The Frogs used their last time out before a run was stuffed. With the clock running, backup quarterback Anthony Sciaraffa hurried onto the field where all confusion promptly broke loose. When he got to the line, he realized the players were in the wrong formation for the play he had called. He couldn't call time out, so he simply took the snap and jumped over the line. Touchdown.

Wacker went for two and the win, sending Gulley in for the pass. Again, confusion broke out. The play was designed to go to Davis in the flat, but he was covered. Under pressure, Gulley spotted Maness and delivered a strike. Despite all the confusion, TCU had a thrilling and downright unbelievable 32-31 win.

Though it sometimes doesn't seem that way, confusion is not the natural order of things. God's universe – from the brilliant arrangement of DNA to the complex harmony of a millipede's legs to the dazzling array of the stars – is ordered. God's act of creation was at its most basic the bringing of order out of chaos.

So why then is confusion so pervasive in our society today? Why do so many of us struggle to make sense of our lives, foundering in our confusion over everything from our morals and values to our sexual orientation and our sense of what is right and what is wrong? The lesson of the Tower of Babel is instructive. That which God does not ordain he does not sustain. Thus, confusion is not the problem itself but is rather a symptom of the absence of God's will and God's power in our lives.

At its most basic, confusion for the children of God is a sense of purposelessness. It fills the void that is created by a lack of intimacy with God.

I saw that [Anthony] Gulley was in trouble and I thought, 'Oh, no, they're gonna get him.'
-- James Maness on the busted play that was the 2-pt. conversion

**In our lives, keeping confusion away
requires keeping God near.**

PLAN AHEAD

Read Psalm 33:1-15.

"The plans of the Lord stand firm forever, the purposes of his heart through all generations" (v. 11).

TCU had a plan against 7th-ranked Oklahoma. It worked.

On Sept. 3, 2005, Gary Patterson's Horned Frogs, coming off a 5-6 season, faced quite a challenge in their season opener in Norman. The Sooners had gone 12-1 in 2004, their only loss to the Trojans of Southern Cal in the Orange Bowl for the national title. They had not lost at home since 2001, and their offense featured sophomore running back Adrian Peterson, the Heisman Trophy runner-up as a freshman. TCU had not beaten a team ranked this high since a 14-6 defeat of No.-7 Baylor in 1960.

But Patterson drew up a game plan that did indeed center on Peterson. It was simple in its conception, tougher in its execution. The Frogs would stop Peterson and make Oklahoma's quarterback beat them in his first career start.

The Frog defense held Peterson to only 63 yards on 22 carries, including five yards on eight carries in the first half. Peterson showed a flash of brilliance with an 11-yard touchdown run on the opening drive of the second half. After that, though, he wasn't a factor.

Thus, just as Patterson planned it, the burden of winning the game fell on Oklahoma's quarterbacks. They weren't up to it.

The game was tied at 10 when the OU quarterback fumbled

while trying to escape junior defensive end Jamison Newby. Linebacker David Hawthorne recovered at the OU 17. Four plays later, Robert Merrill took a pitchout from Tye Gunn, who threw for 226 yards and a touchdown, and scored untouched. The final of 17-10 was on the board with 11:56 left.

Oklahoma had one last chance to save itself, but just as Patterson planned it, a quarterback fumble finished the Sooners off.

In retrospect the game wasn't an upset. TCU went 11-1 with a No.-11 ranking and won the Mountain West Conference championship while Oklahoma stumbled to an 8-4 record.

Successful living takes planning. You go to school to improve your chances for a better paying job. You use blueprints to build your home. You plan for retirement. You map out your vacation to have the best time. You even plan your children -- sometimes.

Your best-laid plans, however, sometime get wrecked by events and circumstances beyond your control. The economy tanks; a debilitating illness strikes; a hurricane hits. Life is capricious and thus no plans -- not even your best ones -- are foolproof.

But you don't have to go it alone. God has plans for your life that guarantee success as God defines it if you will make him your planning partner. God's plan for your life includes joy, love, peace, kindness, gentleness, and faithfulness, all the elements necessary for truly successful living for today and for all eternity. And God's plan will not fail.

A man without a plan doesn't have a future.

-- Gary Patterson

**Your plans may ensure a successful life;
God's plans will ensure a successful eternity.**

A ROARING SUCCESS

Read Galatians 5:16-26.

*"So I say, live by the Spirit. . . . The sinful nature desires
what is contrary to the Spirit. . . . I warn you, as I did
before, that those who live like this will not inherit the
kingdom of God" (vv. 16, 17, 21).*

As unlikely as it may have been, for Ashley Davis, basketball
success at TCU came in threes.

In high school in San Antonio, Davis was a post player whose
inside power and moves earned her all-state honors. She once
said that she could probably count on two hands the number of
three-point shots she launched in high school.

Thus, when Frogs coach Jeff Mittie scouted and recruited Davis,
he was looking for his team's next post player. He had his eyes
on Davis during a summer league game when the team casually
warmed up before the start of the second half. To Mittie's shock,
Davis was bombing threes from all over the court. "She hit like
seven or eight in a row, and I had to do a double-take to make
sure I was really seeing it," Mittie recalled.

He was, but he still wasn't sure about what he had seen. The
first time Mittie talked to Davis on the phone, his first question
was about all those threes he had seen at the summer league
game. "I wanted to make sure it wasn't a fluke," Mittie said.

It wasn't, and when Davis committed to the Lady Frogs, Mittie
set about changing the way she played on the court. It took work,

but Davis was up to it, staying during the summers to practice and to get stronger.

The result was success. When the two-time captain ended her Frog career in 2006-07, she left TCU ranked second in school history in threes with 232, behind only Jill Sutton. She remains the school's seventh-leading scorer with 1,291 points. Her 78 treys her senior season is second all-time to Sutton's 81 in 1997-98.

Are you a successful person? Your answer, of course, depends upon how you define success. Is the measure of your success the number of digits in your bank balance, the square footage of your house, that title on your office door, the size of your boat, or the number of cars in your garage?

Certainly the world determines success by wealth, fame, prestige, awards, and possessions. Our culture screams that life is all about gratifying your own needs and wants. If it feels good, do it. It's basically the Beach Boys' philosophy of life.

But all success of this type has one glaring shortcoming: You can't take it with you. Eventually, Daddy takes the T-bird away. Like life itself, all these things are fleeting.

A more lasting way and rewarding to approach success is through the spiritual rather than the physical. The goal becomes not money or backslaps by sycophants but eternal life spent with God. Success of that kind is forever.

If you coach for 25 years and never win a championship but you influence three people for Christ, that is success.
-- Oklahoma women's basketball coach Sherri Coale

Success isn't permanent, and failure isn't fatal --
unless it's in your relationship with God.

TO TELL THE TRUTH

Read Matthew 5:33-37.

*"Simply let your 'Yes' be 'Yes,' and your 'No,' 'No';
anything beyond this comes from the evil one" (v. 37).*

TCU head coach Dutch Meyer once used a bald-faced lie to motivate his team.

TCU met SMU on Nov. 26, 1949, in what was the last of three duels between a pair of great tailbacks/quarterbacks, TCU's Lindy Berry and the Mustangs' Heisman Trophy winner, Doak Walker. The game also marked the last head-to-head meeting of Meyer and his longtime friend and former assistant, Matty Bell, who was retiring. Meyer found a way to turn the situation to his advantage.

As Berry recalled it, the coach, who was never averse to shedding a tear or two, came into the locker room before the game, "kinda shuffling around and mumbling and gettin' weepy and all." Finally, Meyer said, "Well boys, I . . . I guess this is gonna be my last game." With his voice cracking, he went on. "They haven't renewed my contract . . . so I guess this is it." Then he added the clincher with tears in his eyes. "Boy, I sure would love to beat Matty one more time."

Berry was the captain, so he held a quick team meeting and told his teammates. "Look, we've just got to go out there and win this game for Dutch." Berry said that as a result, "We went out there all fired up."

Berry was the star of the game. In the second quarter, he combined with George Boal for a 56-yard pass and run play that set up a 29-yard touchdown toss to Jimmy Hickey. He scored the second Frog TD on a run and clinched the 21-13 victory with a 21-yard touchdown pass to John Archer.

In the locker room after the game, Meyer used a towel to wipe away more tears but was coy with reporters who asked if this were really his last game. Later in the week, the Frog players learned their devious head coach had signed a new three-year contract two days before the SMU game.

TCU fans may well argue that Dutch Meyer was right in using whatever tools and tricks he could to motivate his Frogs. Generally, though, when we lie, we don't have such altruistic motives in mind. More often than not, rather than lying to spare the feelings of others (No, dear, that dress doesn't make you look fat.), we lie to bail ourselves out of a jam, to make ourselves look better to others, or to gain the upper hand over someone.

But Jesus admonishes us to tell the truth. Frequently in our faith life we fret about what is right and what is wrong, but we can have no such ambivalence when it comes to deciding whether we should tell the truth or lie. God and his son are so closely associated with the truth that lying is ultimately attributed to the devil ("the evil one").

Given his character, God cannot lie; given his character, the devil lies as a way of life. Given your character, which is it?

He never actually gave a straight answer.
  -- Whit Canning on Meyer's being asked if SMU were his last game

**Jesus declared himself to be the truth,
so whose side are we on when we lie?**

UNBELIEVABLE!

Read Hebrews 3:7-19.

"See to it, brothers, that none of you has a sinful, unbelieving heart that turns away from the living God" (v. 12).

What the Frogs did to Kansas was so unbelievable that it sent the numbers wonks scrambling to the record books.

The move to the Big 12 in 2012-13 was not kind to the TCU men's basketball team. After starting the season 9-4 in nonconference play, the Frogs lost their first eight Big 12 games. Few folks around the country had little doubt that the string of losses would get longer when Kansas came to Fort Worth on Wednesday, Feb. 6. As usual, the Jayhawks were in the top 10, ranked No. 5 with a gaudy 19-2 record. The line on the game was 18.5 points.

What happened that night at Daniel-Meyer Coliseum has been described as the program's "all-time greatest upset" and "one of the most improbable upsets in recent college basketball history."

The Frogs beat Kansas -- and it was no fluke.

TCU never trailed; the Frogs scored the game's first eight points and built a 16-point lead halfway through the second half. This was after they had not held more than seven-point lead against a conference foe all season. Kansas hit only one of its first 17 shots and didn't score a point until more than seven minutes into the game. With 6:19 to go in the first half, KU had two points.

Since they couldn't play any worse, the Jayhawks did better

the last half, but it was too late. By then, "TCU believed it could win, and was out-playing" Kansas. A 17-4 run late in the half cut the Frog lead to 44-40, but a layup from Garlon Green with a nice assist from Adrick McKinney ended the free fall. Down the stretch, the Frogs made enough free throws to win 62-55.

The win was so unbelievable that Jerry Palm of *CBSSports.com* tweeted, "In terms of RPI difference between the teams, TCU's win is the biggest upset in the 20 years I've been tracking numbers."

Much of what taxes the limits of our belief system has little effect on our lives. Maybe we don't believe in UFOs, honest politicians, aluminum baseball bats, Sasquatch, or the viability of electric cars. A healthy dose of skepticism is a natural defense mechanism that helps protect us in a world that all too often has designs on taking advantage of us.

That's not the case, however, when Jesus and God are part of the mix. Quite unbelievably, we often hear people blithely assert they don't believe in God. Or brazenly declare they believe in God but don't believe Jesus was anything but a good man and a great teacher.

At this point, unbelief becomes dangerous because God doesn't fool around with scoffers. He locks them out of the Promised Land, which isn't a country in the Middle East but Heaven itself.

Given that scenario, it's downright unbelievable that anyone would not believe.

A frenetic, I-don't-believe-what-I-just-saw moment.
        -- Writer Stefan Stevenson on TCU's win over Kansas

Perhaps nothing is as unbelievable as that some people insist on not believing in God or his son.

SOMETHING NEW

Read Ephesians 4:17-24.

"You were taught . . . to put off your old self . . . and to put on the new self, created to be like God in true righteousness and holiness" (vv. 22, 24).

The national-champion Frogs of 1938 were so good that they encountered something new in the Sugar Bowl: they fell behind.

The 11-0 Frogs boasted two All-Americas in tailback Davey O'Brien, who won the Heisman Trophy, and center-linebacker Ki Aldrich. Only Arkansas at 21-14 stayed within one score of the Frogs during the regular season. The Razorbacks were also the only team to score in double digits against the TCU defense.

The undefeated season and the top ranking in the polls landed TCU in the fifth edition of the Sugar Bowl on Jan. 1. The opponent was the Tartans of Carnegie Tech, which had lost only one game during the season, 7-0 to Notre Dame.

TCU punted just one time the entire game, but it set up the Frogs' first touchdown. Jack Odle's 40-yard punt in the second quarter rolled out of bounds at the Tech 6. The Tartans couldn't move and punted out to their own 48. From there, TCU scored in eleven plays. The touchdown was set up by a fourth-down pass from O'Brien to halfback Johnny Hall down to the 4. Sophomore fullback Connie Sparks, who led the conference in scoring, got the game's first touchdown from the 1 on third down.

But the Frogs missed the extra point, setting them up for a new experience. Carnegie Tech answered with a touchdown drive and a 7-6 lead, the first time the whole season the Frogs had been behind. The team had a new challenge facing it.

Undismayed by the newness of their situation, the Frogs drove 80 yards in the third quarter for the game-winning touchdown. Sophomore end Durwood Horner scored on a 44-yard pass from O'Brien. Tech responded with a drive to the TCU 28, but Aldrich intercepted a pass, and the Tartans never threatened again.

O'Brien added a fourth-quarter field goal that made the final score 15-7. Winning was certainly nothing new for this bunch.

New things in our lives often have a life-changing effect. A new spouse. A new baby. A new job. Even something as mundane as a new television set or lawn mower jolts us with change.

While new experiences, new people, and new toys may make our lives new, they can't make new lives for us. Inside, where it counts – down in the deepest recesses of our soul – we're still the same, no matter how desperately we may wish to change.

An inner restlessness drives us to seek escape from a life that is a monotonous routine. Such a mundane existence just isn't good enough for someone who is a child of God; it can't even be called living. We want more out of life; something's got to change.

The only hope for a new life lies in becoming a brand new man or woman. And that is possible only through Jesus Christ, he who can make all things new again.

The Frogs got off the floor to win.
-- Writer Flem Hall on TCU's coming from behind for the first time

A brand new you with the promise
of a life worth living is waiting in Jesus Christ.

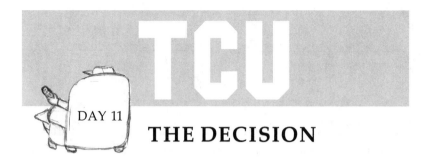

THE DECISION

Read John 6:60-69.

"The words I have spoken to you are spirit and they are life. Yet there are some of you who do not believe" (vv. 63b-64a).

With time running out, TCU head coach Abe Martin made a daring and risky decision that helped the Frogs pull off one of their greatest upsets ever.

On Sept. 28, 1957, the Horned Frogs took on an Ohio State Buckeye team generally hailed as one of the best in the country. Most of the experts pegged TCU as a two-to-three touchdown underdog, but the Frogs certainly didn't play like it.

TCU took the opening kickoff and drove 58 yards for a touchdown. Sophomore Marvin Lasater, who had moved into the starting lineup during the week, went eight yards for the score. Ohio State answered with a 77-yard drive to take a 7-6 lead. On the first play of the second quarter, All-SWC halfback Jim Shofner sprinted down the sideline for a 90-yard touchdown on a punt return. Again, the Buckeyes answered and led 14-12 at halftime.

Early in the third quarter, end Chico Mendoza fell on an Ohio State fumble at the 31. Fullback Jack Spikes then ripped straight ahead for a 16-yard touchdown and an 18-14 TCU lead.

With only 2:40 to play, Ohio State had driven 50 yards to the TCU 33. The starters were obviously tiring, and when senior guard John Groom was injured, Martin took advantage of the delay to make his decision. Incredibly, he pulled his starters and sent in the entire second team. OSU moved to the 21, but then Don Floyd, who would be an All-American end, and end Bill Roach jarred the ball loose from the Buckeye running back. All-SWC linebacker Dale Walker (1958) recovered at the 28.

TCU ran out the clock for the 18-14 win, Ohio State's only loss of the season. Not only was Martin's decision unusual but so was the fact that the Frogs did not complete a pass the entire game.

As with Abe Martin, the decisions you have made along the way have shaped your life at every pivotal moment. Some decisions you made suddenly and carelessly; some you made carefully and deliberately; some were forced upon you. You may have discovered that some of those spur-of-the-moment decisions have turned out better than your carefully considered ones.

Of all your life's decisions, however, none is more important than one you cannot ignore: What have you done with Jesus? Even in his time, people chose to follow Jesus or to reject him, and nothing has changed; the decision must still be made and nobody can make it for you. Ignoring Jesus won't work either; that is, in fact, a decision, and neither he nor the consequences of your decision will go away.

Carefully considered or spontaneous – how you arrive at a decision for Jesus doesn't matter; all that matters is that you get there.

If you make a decision that you think is the proper one at the time, then that's the correct decision.

-- John Wooden

A decision for Jesus may be spontaneous or considered; what counts is that you make it.

ON CALL

Read 1 Samuel 3:1-18.

"The Lord came and stood there, calling as at the other times, 'Samuel! Samuel!' Then Samuel said, 'Speak, for your servant is listening'" (v. 10).

Gary Patterson had no choice. To avoid a season-wrecking loss, he had to call on an unproven, untested freshman.

Expectations were high when the 22nd-ranked Horned Frogs opened the 2006 season on the road against Baylor. They wound up in deep trouble early on, though. The first half ended with the Bears leading 7-0, and for the Frogs, it got worse at halftime.

Senior quarterback Jeff Ballard, the team's 2005 MVP who was 8-0 as a starter, completed 7-of-14 passes for 85 yards in the first half. He took some hard hits, though, and was so woozy at halftime that Patterson was forced to sit him down. That left the head Frog scrambling for a replacement.

All he could find was Marcus Jackson, a redshirt freshman who had not played a single down as a collegiate quarterback. "He was the only person we had left," Patterson admitted. "It was either going to be him or me throwing." Jackson had been projected as the third-string quarterback, but expected senior backup Chad Huffman signed a pro baseball contract. Before the season, the coaches warned Jackson that he might be called on.

Just before the second half began, Patterson made the call. "Coach told me in the summer I had a good chance to play, and in two-a-days needed to practice like I would play," Jackson said. "I took his word and I was ready."

Indeed he was. Jackson threw for 148 yards and two touchdowns in the last half to lead the Frogs to a 17-7 win that avoided what would have been a devastating loss. He put TCU ahead with an 84-yard touchdown pass to tailback Aaron Brown in the third quarter and then clinched the game with a 4-yard flip to tight end Quinton Cunigan in the final period.

Jackson answered the call so well that he was named the Mountain West Conference Offensive Player of the Week.

A team player is someone who does whatever the coach calls upon him to do for the good of the team. Something quite similar occurs when God places a specific call upon a Christian's life.

Such a call is much scarier, though, than entering a football game unexpectedly as Marcus Jackson did. The way many folks under-stand it is that answering God's call means going into the ministry, packing the family up, and moving halfway around the world to some place where folks have never heard of air conditioning, fried chicken, paved roads, or the Horned Frogs. Zambia. The Philippines. Cleveland even.

Not for you, no thank you. And who can blame you?

But God usually calls folks to serve him where they are. In fact, God put you where you are right now, and he has a purpose in placing you there. Wherever you are, you are called to serve him.

It was crazy. I had a couple of warmup throws, maybe three or four.
— Marcus Jackson on answering the sudden call to play vs. Baylor

God calls you to serve him right now
right where he has put you, wherever that is.

DAY 13

CALLING IT QUITS

Read Numbers 13:25-14:4.

"The men who had gone up with him said, 'We can't attack those people; they are stronger than we are'" (v. 13:31).

Calli Corley learned that she really did love volleyball -- but only after she quit the sport twice.

Corley was a basketball and track star in high school who also played volleyball for three years while she waited for hoops or track to start up. When she graduated, she knew she wanted to attend TCU but wasn't at all interested in playing volleyball.

So she gave up the sport and came to TCU in the fall of 2003 as a regular student. Along the way, though, TCU's head coach, Prentice Lewis, heard of Corley's talent and encouraged her to walk on. "I didn't want to at first," Corley said. "I just wasn't sure that was how I wanted to spend my first year." But she tried out, made the team, and saw action in 25 matches.

It didn't feel right, though. So for the second time, Corley quit the sport, this time to concentrate on her sorority during her sophomore year. She even considered transferring to escape volleyball entirely. Again, though, something didn't feel quite right. "I just wasn't ready to say that's it for good," Corley said.

In the fall of 2005, she decided to give volleyball another try. She went to Lewis and begged her for another chance. The head coach was wary. "I wanted her back, but [Corley] needed to prove she wanted to be with us," Lewis said. "She had to earn her way back."

Corley did just that. In quitting volleyball, she discovered how much she loved the game. She earned a scholarship and was a full-time starter her last two seasons. When she finished up in 2007, Corley held the school record with 1,406 digs, shattering the previous record of 1,197 held by Marci King (1998-2001).

Not too shabby for a walk-on who twice quit the sport.

Remember that time you quit a sports team as Calli Corley did at TCU? That night you bailed out of a relationship? Walked away from a job with the goals unachieved? Sometimes quitting is the most sensible way to minimize your losses, so you may well at times in your life give up on something or someone.

In your relationship with God, however, you should remember the people of Israel, who quit when the Promised Land was theirs for the taking. They forgot one fact of life you never should: God never gives up on you.

That means you should never, ever give up on God. No matter how tired or discouraged you get, no matter that it seems your prayers aren't getting through to God, no matter what – quitting on God is not an option.

He is preparing a blessing for you, and in his time, he will bring it to fruition -- if you don't quit on him.

I think I needed to live without volleyball to realize that I couldn't live without volleyball.
-- Calli Corley on what she learned when she quit the sport

Whatever else you give up on in your life, don't quit on God; he will never ever give up on you.

LANGUAGE BARRIER

Read Mark 16:9-20.

"Go into all the world and preach the good news to all creation" (v. 13).

No matter what the locals may call it, Ryan Christian has scored a touchdown wherever he's played.

From 2006-09, Christian was a wide receiver and running back for the Frogs. He appeared in 47 games with eight starts and lettered all four years, accumulating 1,859 yards and scoring nine touchdowns. When TCU's 2010 Pro Day rolled around, Christian had a shot at getting a serious look from the NFL until he caught the flu. "I knew I wasn't going to perform my best if I showed up, so I decided not to go," he said.

Christian signed with the Toronto Argonauts of the Canadian Football League for the 2010 season and put his name in the team's record book when he returned a kickoff 110 yards for a touchdown (or a *major* as its known). After the season, he returned to Fort Worth to work as an intern with Christ Chapel church.

Christian's football days seemed behind him until he received an email from a coach of a pro team in Parma, Italy, who had heard of him from a former TCU offensive coordinator. On March 23, 2013, he played his first game in a Parma uniform. It also marked his first-ever appearance at quarterback when the starter broke his hand on a helmet. "It was pretty interesting," Christian said.

He played before a few hundred die-hard fans instead of the

50,000-or-so fanatics he was accustomed to at TCU and was paid only $770 per week. Still, Christian was content because he felt he was right where the Lord put him. When he crossed the goal line in that first game in Italy, Christian's odyssey meant that he had scored a touchdown in three countries. To him, though, "a touchdown has the same meaning in any language."

Our games don't always translate across national and cultural boundaries. Language, though, is what usually erects a barrier to understanding. Recall your overseas vacation or your call to a tech support number when you got someone who spoke English but didn't understand it. Talking loud and waving your hands doesn't facilitate communication; it just makes you look weird.

Like many other aspects of life, faith has its jargon that can sometimes hinder understanding. Sanctification, justification, salvation, Advent, Communion with its symbolism of eating flesh and drinking blood – these and many other words have specific meanings to Christians that may be incomprehensible, confusing, and downright daunting to the newcomer or the seeker.

But the heart of Christianity's message centers on words that require no explanation: words such as hope, joy, love, purpose, and community. Their meanings are universal because people the world over seek them in their lives. Nobody speaks that language better than Jesus does.

Kindness is the universal language that all people understand.
-- Legendary Florida A&M coach Jake Gaither

Jesus speaks across all language barriers
because his message of hope and meaning
resounds with people everywhere.

HOMELESS

Read Matthew 8:18-22.

"Jesus replied, 'Foxes have holes and birds of the air have nests, but the Son of Man has no place to lay his head'" (v. 20).

For almost two decades, TCU marched through "realignment wilderness"; in effect, the Frogs were homeless. Finally, in October 2011, they came home.

The seismic waves of conference shifting hit TCU hard in 1994 when the old Southwest Conference fell apart. For 72 years, TCU had called the venerable conference home. Seemingly overnight, however, Texas, Texas A&M, Texas Tech, and Baylor left Houston, Rice, SMU, and TCU behind for the Big 12. The SWC was dead.

As difficult as it was to swallow, the big boys of college football didn't want TCU. In 2012, Andy Staples of *Sports Illustrated* wrote, "People at TCU still stew about getting abandoned." Some, like Dick Lowe, a guard for Dutch Meyer from 1947-50, said TCU should have seen the kick to the curb coming. "We deserved to be kicked out," he said. "We weren't carrying our end of the load."

Desperate for a home, TCU began an "extraordinary journey through the conference landscape of college athletics" that would take them into five different conferences. The Frogs landed in the Western Athletic Conference in 1996. In October 2001, they moved into a slightly better neighborhood with Conference USA.

When TCU went 21-4 in 2002 and '03, the Mountain West, which had previously shunned them, offered the Frogs yet another new home. TCU continued winning and moved back into the big time with a decision in November 2010 to move to the Big East.

The Frogs never played a game there. When Texas A&M left the Big 12 for the SEC, the league called. On Oct. 10, 2011, TCU officially joined the Big 12. The Frogs were home, back where they belonged with some of the gang from the old neighborhood.

Rock bottom in America has a face: the bag lady pushing a shopping cart; the scruffy guy with a beard and a backpack at the interstate exit holding a cardboard sign. Look closer at that bag lady or that scruffy guy, though, and you may see desperate women with children fleeing violence, veterans haunted by their combat experiences, or sick or injured workers.

Few of us are indifferent to the homeless when we pass by them or they accost us on the street. They often raise quite strong passions, whether we regard them as a ministry or an odorous nuisance. They trouble us, perhaps because we realize that we're only one catastrophic illness and a few paychecks away from joining them on the pavement. They remind us of how tenuous our own holds upon material success really are.

But the homeless people on our streets and under our overpasses should also stir our compassion because they are children of the Lord we serve, who – like them -- had no home.

TCU has traveled a long path, been to different places. I'd like to welcome you home.

-- Big 12 interim commissioner Chuck Neinas

**Because they, too, are God's children,
the homeless merit our compassion, not our scorn.**

GOOD LUCK

Read Acts 1:15-25.

"Then they prayed, 'Lord, you know everyone's heart. Show us which of these two you have chosen.' . . . Then they cast lots" (vv. 24, 25a).

Were the Frogs lucky or good on one of the most legendary plays in school football history? Probably some of both.

With two minutes left in the 2011 Rose Bowl, the Wisconsin Badgers lined up to save themselves. TCU had taken its opening possession of the second half and driven for a touchdown on Luke Shivers' 1-yard run. That gave the Frogs a 21-13 lead in the biggest game in the school's modern football history.

But the Badgers put together a 77-yard drive in the game's waning minutes and scored with exactly two minutes to play. 21-19. The Frogs' coaching staff knew what to expect on the 2-point conversion for the tie. Wisconsin would do what it did best: run the ball behind its dominant offensive line.

The Badgers had other plans. They lined up in a spread, a shot-gun formation with four wide receivers. The Frogs had a double blitz on with a linebacker and a safety racing in. As the play unfolded -- one of the biggest, if not the biggest, in TCU football history -- the defense was a disaster.

A mistake in the Frogs' secondary left a Wisconsin receiver wide open in the end zone. To make the fiasco worse, linebacker Tank Carder's blitz attempt never happened; he got stuffed at the line. "I went to go blitz and got blocked and couldn't get through the hole," he explained.

So he stopped. Knowing he couldn't get to the quarterback, Carder took a step back from his blocker and jumped. He wound up in the right place at the right time and knocked down the pass attempt to preserve the win and the undefeated season.

As ESPN's Brian Bennett put it, "the Horned Frogs are lucky Carder is so good."

Ever think sometimes that other people have all the luck? Some guy wins a lottery while you can't get a raise of a few lousy bucks at work. The football takes a lucky bounce the other team's way and TCU loses a game. If you have any luck to speak of, it's bad.

To ascribe anything that happens in life to blind luck, however, is to believe that random chance controls everything, including you. But here's the truth: Luck exists only as a makeshift explanation for something beyond our ken. When the apostles in effect flipped a coin to pick the new guy, they acknowledged that the lots merely revealed to them a decision God had already made.

It's true that we can't explain why some people skate merrily through life while others suffer in horrifying ways. We don't know why good things happen to bad people and vice versa. But none of it results from luck, unless, as the disciples did, you want to attribute that name to the force that does indeed control the universe; you know -- the one more commonly called God.

We were lucky Tank [Carder] was in the game.
-- TCU head coach Gary Patterson

A force does exist that is in charge of your life,
but it isn't luck; it's God.

THE LONG SHOTS

Read Matthew 9:9-13.

*"[Jesus] saw a man named Matthew sitting at the tax
collector's booth. 'Follow me,' he told him, and Matthew
got up and followed him" (v. 9).*

To keep their season alive, the Frogs had to win four straight
games, including two over a team that had just beaten them. They
were, to say the least, long shots.

After a 6-2 loss to Ole Miss in the opening round of the 2012
regional at College Station, TCU was at the bottom looking up
in the four-team, double elimination tournament; one defeat and
they were gone. These long shots figured, though, that they may
as well give it their best shot.

First off was an elimination game against Dayton. The situation
was pretty dire when the Flyers led 9-6 after five innings. The
Frogs then pulled off something veteran head coach Jim Schlossnagle had never seen before. Over the last four innings, they
scored 22 runs to win 28-12, the fifth-most runs ever scored in
the NCAA Tournament. Eight TCU players had multi-hit games;
freshman Jerrick Suiter had five hits. Senior outfielder Brance
Rivera was on base four times, scored four runs, and drove in
six. He had a grand slam during the Frogs' nine-run ninth inning.
TCU also scored seven runs in the sixth and six in the seventh.

"I think today showed just how well we can take a blow and
come right back from it," Rivera said. "From here on out, it's an

elimination game, and we have to play like it."

And so the long shots did. After that remarkable game, TCU scored only a pedestrian ten runs in a 10-2 rout of Texas A&M and was downright calm in a 5-2 win over Ole Miss that forced a one-game playoff. In that situation, TCU wasn't a long shot anymore. The Frogs were, in fact, dead even with the Rebels.

They completed the four-game comeback by winning 7-4. It was on to the Super Regional for the long-shot Frogs.

Like TCU in the 2012 regional, Matthew the tax collector was a long shot. In his case, he was an unlikely person to be a confidant of the Son of God. While we may not get all warm and fuzzy about the IRS, our government's revenue agents are nothing like Matthew and his ilk. He bought a franchise, paying the Roman Empire for the privilege of extorting, bullying, and stealing everything he could from his own people. Tax collectors of the time were "despicable, vile, unprincipled scoundrels."

And yet, Jesus said only two words to this lowlife: "Follow me." Jesus knew that this long shot would make an excellent disciple.

It's the same with us. While we may not be quite as vile as Matthew was, none of us can stand before God with our hands clean and our hearts pure. We are all impossibly long shots to enter God's Heaven. That is, until we do what Matthew did: get up and follow Jesus.

You get your back pressed against the wall, you find out about people a little bit.

-- Jim Schlossnagle on his 2012 Frogs in the regional

**Jesus changes us from being long shots
to enter God's Kingdom to being sure things.**

DAY 18

TEARS IN HEAVEN

Read Revelation 21:1-8.

"[God] will wipe every tear from their eyes. There will be no more death or mourning or crying or pain" (v. 4).

What the Frogs did drove their head coach to tears.

For 51 minutes on Oct. 20, 1951, TCU's game with Texas A&M went exactly as the pundits had predicted. The undefeated and 6th-ranked Aggies dominated the 2-2 Horned Frogs and led 14-0. TCU struggled on offense without its preseason All-American quarterback, Gilbert Bartosh, injured the week before. Moreover, backup tailback Mal Fowler and fullback Bobby Jack Floyd were also sidelined by injuries. Left to lead the team was sophomore Ray McKown.

With nine minutes left, McKown took a deep snap and broke down the sideline for a 49-yard touchdown run. On the successful PAT, the Aggies roughed the kicker. With the 15-yard penalty assessed on the kickoff, head coach Dutch Meyer and assistant coach Allie White decided to gamble on an onside kick.

TCU's Wayne Martin fell on the ball at the A&M 30, and the Frogs quickly drove for a touchdown. The extra point was no good, though, leaving the score at 14-13 with time running out.

TCU then got a big break. On the second play after the kickoff, A&M fumbled, and future TCU Hall-of-Fame member Roy Pitcock got the ball. With 1:35 left to play, McKown made it into the end zone, and TCU had an incredible 20-14 win in a game consistently ranked among the greatest in Frog history.

Meyer certainly thought so. He was so overcome he collapsed into sobs afterwards. "This was the sweetest victory of my coaching career," he declared, "and the most courageous comeback I've ever witnessed."

The legendary coach would have a lot to cry about that season. Behind All-American seasons from McKown and tackle Doug Conaway, the team rallied from that slow start to win Meyer's third Southwest Conference championship.

When your parents died. When a friend told you she was divorcing. When you broke your collarbone as a child. When you watch a sad movie.

You cry. Crying is as much a part of life as are breathing, overpriced movie popcorn, and potholes on the highway. Usually our tears are brought on by pain, sorrow, or disappointment.

But what about when your child was born? When TCU wins? When you discovered Jesus Christ? Those times elicit tears too; we cry at the times of our greatest, most overwhelming joy.

Thus, while there will be tears in Heaven, they will only be tears of sheer, unmitigated, undiluted joy. The greatest joy possible, a joy beyond our imagining, must occur when we finally see Christ. If we shed tears when the Frogs win a game, can we really believe that we will stand dry-eyed and calm in the presence of Jesus?

What we will not shed in Heaven are tears of sorrow and pain.

Are you crying? There's no crying, there's no crying in baseball.
    -- Tom Hanks as Jimmy Dugan in A League of Their Own

**Tears in Heaven will be like everything else there:
a part of the joy we will experience.**

RUN FOR IT

Read John 20:1-10.

"Peter and the other disciple started for the tomb. Both were running, but the other disciple outran Peter and reached the tomb first" (vv. 3-4).

No one in the history of college football has ever run with the ball as LaDainian Tomlinson did one glorious afternoon.

Tomlinson spent his first two seasons at TCU splitting time with Basil Mitchell. As a junior in 1999, he led the NCAA in rushing with 1,850 yards. His senior season he again was the nation's leading rusher and was first-team All-America. He won the Doak Walker Award as the nation's best running back and was fourth in the voting for the Heisman Trophy.

In 1998, Tomlinson helped the Frogs to a 7-5 season that ended with a 28-19 win over Southern Cal in the Sun Bowl. The bowl was the Frogs' first since 1994 and second since 1984, so trips to a bowl game were not the regular occurrence they are now.

Thus, when the Horned Frogs took on Texas El-Paso on Nov. 20, 1999, at home, the game was a significant one. A win would be the Frogs' sixth of the season, making them bowl eligible. (They would win eight games, including a 28-14 whipping of East Carolina in the Mobile Alabama Bowl.)

Tomlinson was therefore quite serious when he said, "Going into the game, I wasn't thinking about a lot of yards. All I was thinking about was winning the game."

The Frogs did win the game -- and Tomlinson did get "a lot of yards." He got 406 of them, in fact, the most in the history of major college football, and a record that still stands. (The previous record was 396 yards set by Tony Sands of Kansas.) He broke the 400-yard barrier with a 7-yard run on his 43rd and final carry.

Along the way, Tomlinson scored six touchdowns in the 52-24 win. He had 287 yards in the last half, touching the ball on 29 of TCU's 37 plays. Fourth-quarter touchdown runs of 70 and 63 yards on consecutive carries put Tomlinson in position to run for the record.

Hit the ground running -- every morning that's what you do as you leave the house and re-enter the rat race. You run errands; you run though a presentation; you give someone a run for his money; you always want to be in the running and never run-of-the-mill.

You're always running toward something, such as your goals, or away from something, such as your past. Many of us spend much of our lives foolishly attempting to run away from God, the purposes he has for us, and the blessings he is waiting to give us.

No matter how hard or how far you run, though, you can never outrun yourself or God. God keeps pace with you, calling you in the short run to take care of the long run by falling to your knees and running for your life -- to Jesus -- just as Peter and the other disciple ran that first Easter morning.

On your knees, you run all the way to glory.

If he's so close to something like that, you've got to let him finish it off.
-- Head coach Dennis Franchione on Tomlinson and the record

You can run to eternity by going to your knees.

JUGGERNAUT

Read Revelation 20.

"Fire came down from heaven and devoured them. And the devil, who deceived them, was thrown into the lake of burning sulfur, where the beast and the false prophet had been thrown" (vv. 9b-10a).

The Baylor Bears were 2-0 and riding high -- and then they ran into a full-fledged juggernaut.

Everybody short of ESPN's Lee Corso -- who had predicted that Oregon State would beat TCU by three touchdowns in the season opener -- knew that the Horned Frogs were pretty darned good in 2010. After they whipped Oregon State 30-21 and buried Tennessee Tech 62-7, they were ranked fourth in the nation. But were they *that* good or were they simply feeling the pollsters' love left over from the sensational 12-1 season of 2009?

The Baylor game would tell. Head coach Gary Patterson was concerned. He had barely stepped out of the shower after the Tech win before his laptop was up and running with tape of the Bears. "We have to be ready to play," he said of the Baylor game. We need "to start acting like the fourth-ranked team in the nation."

Well, on Sept. 18 at home, the Frogs didn't play like the No.-4 ranked team in the country. They played better than that. They unleashed a juggernaut on the unsuspecting Bears and crushed them 45-3 -- and the game wasn't really that close.

Baylor was helpless against the TCU offense, especially in the first half. Andy Dalton completed his first eleven passes, and TCU scored touchdowns on its first five possessions. The first four drives went 80, 73, 73, and 90 yards. The offense was so effective that the longest drive took only 4 minutes and 7 seconds.

Overall, the Frogs rolled up 578 yards of offense and led 35-3 at halftime. That domination made it easy for the defense, which held Baylor to 263 total yards, 176 of which came after halftime when the game was over.

On this day, the Frogs showed just how good they really were.

Maybe your personal experience with a juggernaut involved a game against a team full of major college prospects, a league tennis match against a former college player, or your presentation for the project you knew didn't stand a chance. Whatever it was, you've been slam-dunked before.

Being part of a juggernaut is much more fun than being in the way of one. Just ask Baylor about that 2010 game. Or consider the forces of evil aligned against God. At least the teams that took the field against the Frogs in 2010 had some hope, however slim, that they might win. No such hope exists for those who oppose God.

That's because their fate is already spelled out in detail. It's in the book; we all know how the story ends. God's enemies may talk big and bluster now, but they will be soundly trounced and routed in the most decisive defeat of all time.

You sure want to be on the winning side in that one.

I wasn't surprised.
      -- Gary Patterson on his team's offensive performance vs. Baylor

**The most lopsided victory in all of history
will be God's ultimate triumph over evil.**

GOOD ADVICE

Read Isaiah 8:11-9:7.

"And he will be called Wonderful Counselor" (v. 9:6b).

Celeste Green received some advice from her coach that she was reluctant to follow. When she did, she had the most successful season of any shooter in TCU rifle history to that point.

In terms of results, TCU's rifle program is the school's strongest of any of its sports teams. Since 2007, the team has never finished lower than fifth in the NCAA championships. The shooters won national titles in 2010 and 2012 and finished third in 2011 and 2013.

Green was one of the best shooters in the program's early years. As a freshman in 2003, she was All-America. After that, though, she had a rocky road at TCU. The house where she lived with her sister burned. Financial troubles and a run-in with her coach forced her to leave school. She eventually landed at West Point, but her troubles continued with physical problems that resulted in a medical discharge. She finished the school year at a junior college, not touching a rifle for twelve months.

New TCU head coach Karen Monez knew Green was out there and that she could help the team. She called Green and asked her to come back and try her fortune at TCU again. Green did.

Her attitude about shooting, though, didn't sit well with her new coach. The sport is generally described as "95 percent mental," and Green didn't approach it that way. Before competitions, she would walk around laughing, talking and joking. Monez advised her to be more focused, to concentrate more before she shot.

Green wasn't interested at first, but Monez had never let her down, so she took the advice. As a senior in 2006, Green became the first Horned Frog shooter to reach the national competition. She finished tenth at the NCAA Championships.

Like Celeste Green, we all need a little advice now and then. More often than not, we turn to professional counselors, who are seemingly everywhere. Marriage counselors, grief counselors, guidance counselors in our schools, rehabilitation counselors, all sorts of mental health and addiction counselors -- We even have pet counselors. No matter what our situation or problem, we can find plenty of advice for the taking.

The problem, of course, is that we find advice easy to offer but hard to swallow. We also have a rueful tendency to solicit the wrong source for advice, seeking counsel that doesn't really solve our problem but that instead enables us to continue with it.

Our need for outside advice, for an independent perspective on our situation, is actually God-given. God serves many functions in our lives, but one role clearly delineated in his Word is that of Counselor. Jesus himself is described as the "Wonderful Counselor." All the advice we need in our lives is right there for the asking; we don't even have to pay for it except with our faith. God is always there for us: to listen, to lead, and to guide.

Basically, [Monez] took me and broke me down and built me back up.
-- Celeste Green on taking her coach's advice

We all need and seek advice in our lives,
but the ultimate and most wonderful Counselor
is of divine and not human origin.

DAY 22

LESSON LEARNED

Read Psalm 143.

"Teach me to do your will, for you are my God" (v. 10).

TCU coach Dick Bumpas had only a few seconds to teach a lesson, but junior Jason Verrett was a quick learner. The result was a game-saving play.

On Nov. 4, 2012, TCU and West Virginia, the two Big 12 rookies, established an immediate rivalry by battling in one of the most exciting games in the Frogs' football history. WVU apparently had the game won with a 76-yard punt return for a touchdown with only 3:19 on the clock.

But the Frogs pulled off a miracle. With 1:28 left, Trevone Boykin hit senior wide receiver Josh Boyce, the team's leading pass catcher, and he outran the Mountaineer defense for a stunning 94-yard touchdown that tied the game at 31. Overtime.

It didn't go well for the Frogs. They missed a field goal, giving WVU a chance to win with a 36-yard kick of its own. That's when Bumpas, the Frogs' defensive coordinator, took advantage of a timeout to teach his lesson.

Studying films in preparation for the game, Bumpas had seen something on WVU's field goal tries that the Frogs could exploit. He took Verrett aside, even though his junior All-American cornerback had never blocked a kick.

He told Verrett that the WVU tight end just kind of stuck his hands out to block on kicks. If Verrett could get under the player's hands and stretch his arms out, he could get a block. Verrett did just that, dashing in from the right side and getting his left hand up for the block that sent the game into a second overtime.

When wide receiver Brandon Carter passed to tight end Corey Fuller on a reverse that went for a 25-yard touchdown and Boyce hauled in Boykins' pass for a two-point conversion, TCU had a 39-38 win. The Frogs got the chance to win only because Dick Bumpas taught a lesson and Jason Verrett learned it.

Learning about anything in life requires a combination of education and experience. Education is the accumulation of facts that we call knowledge; experience is the acquisition of wisdom and discernment, which add purpose and understanding to our knowledge. Education without experience just doesn't have much practical value in our world today.

The most difficult way to learn is trial and error: dive in blindly and mess up. The best way to learn is through example coupled with a set of instructions: Someone has gone ahead to show you the way and has written down the information you need to follow.

In teaching us the way to live godly lives, God chose the latter method. He set down in his book the habits, actions, and attitudes that make for a way of life in accordance with his wishes. He also sent us Jesus to explain and to illustrate.

God teaches us not only how to exist but how to live. We just need to be attentive students.

Coach Bump pulled me aside and said, 'We need a big play right here.'
— Jason Verrett on his game-saving block vs. WVU

To learn from Jesus is to learn what life is all about and how God means for us to live it.

DREAM WORLD

Read Joshua 3.

"All Israel passed by until the whole nation had completed the crossing on dry ground" (v. 17b).

Hayes Rydel pursued his dream to the point of tackling trees.

Rydel's lifelong dream was to play big-time college football, but as a 190-lb. nose guard in high school, he simply wasn't big enough. He played two years at a junior college and didn't start.

Rydel decided to walk on at TCU, so he began training in a rather unique way. He donned full pads and used the trees in a park in Arlington as tackling dummies. "I'd get a running start of about 10 yards, wrap 'em up or practice spin moves," he recalled. "And you know what? They're very stable."

TCU head football coach Pat Sullivan heard about Rydel and advised him that "he would be much more likely to make the team if he was actually enrolled at the school." The day Rydel was admitted to TCU, Sullivan gave him a tryout. When Rydel walked into the locker room, a player greeted him with "Hey, man, can I have a towel?" The Frog thought he was a student trainer.

On Aug. 19, 1994, Rydel trotted out for his first-ever big-time college football practice. He immediately found himself lined up against the Frogs' "orneriest fullback," Koi Woods, in what was called the "gauntlet drill." "He came right at me and tried to bowl me over," Rydel said. "I did the best I could, and he went backward. I was like, Yeah, this is my team."

HORNED FROGS

Five days after he flattened Woods (the back, not the trees), Rydel was awarded a scholarship. First-string nose guard Brian Brooks broke his leg in the '94 opener; Rydel went in and had 13 tackles. He started the next week and didn't leave the lineup for the next two seasons. He was a team captain as a senior in 1995.

"I haven't always started, but I certainly have never quit," Rydel said about making his dream come true.

No matter how tightly or doggedly we cling to our dreams, devotion to them won't make them a reality. Moreover, the cold truth is that all too often dreams don't come true, even when we put forth a mighty effort. The realization of our dreams generally results from a head-on collision of persistence and timing.

But what if our dreams don't come true because they're not the same dreams God has for us? That is, they're not good enough and, in many cases, they're not big enough.

God calls us to great achievements because God's dreams for us are greater than our dreams for ourselves. Could the Israelites, wallowing in the misery of slavery, even dream of a land of their own? Could they imagine actually going to such a place?

The fulfillment of such great dreams occurs only when our dreams and God's will for our lives are the same. Our dreams should be worthy of our best – and worthy of God's involvement in making them come true.

I needed a scholarship, and I didn't want to sit the bench. I have my dreams.

-- Hayes Rydel

**If our dreams are to come true, they
must be worthy of God's involvement in them.**

DAY 24

NO APOLOGIES

Read Acts 4:1-21.

"For we cannot help speaking about what we have seen and heard" (v. 20).

TCU was so dominant against Tennessee Tech that head coach Gary Patterson apologized for his team's last touchdown.

On Sept. 11, 2010, the 4th-ranked Horned Frogs were heavily favored over Tennessee Tech of the Football Championship Subdivision. They dominated from the start. On the team's first possession, Andy Dalton hit sophomore wide receiver Josh Boyce with a 24-yard touchdown pass. When senior cornerback Jason Teague returned an interception 29 yards for a score, TCU led 21-0 in the first quarter.

By halftime, the score was 35-7. A 27-0 last half put the final of 62-7 on the scoreboard, the most points TCU had scored since whipping Stephen F. Austin 67-7 in the second week of the 2008 season. "We did have some mistakes," Dalton declared. Patterson agreed. "I'm not unhappy," he said, "but we have some [issues] we need to make sure we take care of." Not many, though. The Frogs outgained Tech 452 yards to 150 in the easy win.

The last TCU touchdown came with 4:09 to play. Fifth-year senior fullback Ryan Hightower, playing in just the fourth game of his career, cut around the left side and suddenly found himself with nothing but 16 yards of open space.

Patterson began his postgame press conference by apologizing

HORNED FROGS

for that score. "We don't do style points," he declared. He pointed out that the Frogs didn't throw a single pass in the fourth quarter. The play on which Hightower scored was designed to pick up a couple of yards, but he cut back and scored. Still, Patterson said, "I'm happy for him."

Nobody was apologizing, though, for the dominant Frog performance, which gave clear indications of good things to come.

We usually apologize when we wrong or injure another person whether it's bumping into someone in the supermarket, causing an automobile accident, or being uncharacteristically harsh or cruel. Courtesy, forthrightness, our sense of justice, and our Christ-centered desire to repair the damage we've done to a relationship demand apologies from us sometime.

But too many Christians in the increasingly hostile environment that is contemporary America find themselves apologizing for their faith and the temerity they display in inviting someone to church or saying the name of Jesus in public. We shouldn't. To apologize for our faith is to declare, in effect, that we are ashamed of Jesus.

Like Peter and John, we do not have to tell anyone we're sorry for our faith or abashedly try to excuse our actions in the name of Christ. We are Christians, heart and soul. And don't those who purposely flaunt their behavior in Christians' faces tell us, "If you don't like it, live with it"? We're just doing the same. Only in our case, we're talking about living eternally.

I want to publicly apologize. I didn't mean to score the last touchdown.
-- Gary Patterson after the Tennessee Tech game

We should never apologize for Jesus.

WINNER'S CIRCLE

Read 1 John 5:1-12.

"Who is it that overcomes the world? Only he who believes that Jesus is the Son of God" (v. 5).

Billy Tubbs was a winner.

He showed up at TCU in 1994 known as a coach "who builds college basketball programs." His record backed up that reputation. In his eighteen seasons at Lamar and Oklahoma, he had had only two losing campaigns, his first year at each school. His resume listed fourteen seasons of 20 wins or more, four Big Eight Conference titles, and a national runner-up finish in 1988.

TCU needed him. The men's program had suffered through a pair of seasons with a combined record of 13-40 that included a total of five conference wins.

When Tubbs arrived, he made no promises about how many games his teams would win. Instead, he promised Billyball, saying his team would "play hard every minute of the game." That had been his trademark at both Lamar and Oklahoma with his squads rolling up the points on offense and pressing the length of the court on defense.

The results were immediate. Tubbs' first team went 16-11. His third team 1996-97, was the first of his four at TCU to win 20 or more games. The apex of his tenure in Fort Worth came in 1997-98 when the Frogs set a school record with 27 wins and went undefeated (14-0) in the WAC. They were ranked No. 15 by the AP and earned the school's first bid to the NCAA Tournament since the 1986-87 season under Jim Killingsworth.

Tubbs stayed at TCU for eight seasons and never had a losing year, winning at least sixteen games every time. His 156 wins is second all-time only to Byron "Buster" Brannon, who won 205 games in nineteen seasons from 1949-67.

What Billy Tubbs did most of all at TCU was win.

Life itself, not just athletic events, is a competition. You vie against other job applicants. You seek admission to a college with a limited number of open spots. You compete against others for a date. Sibling rivalry is real; just ask your brother or sister.

Inherent in any competition or in any situation that involves wining and losing is an antagonist. You always have an opponent to overcome, even if it's an inanimate video game, a golf course, or even yourself.

Nobody wants to be numbered among life's losers. We recognize them when we see them, and maybe mutter a prayer that says something like, "There but for the grace of God go I."

But one adversary will defeat us: Death will claim us all. We can turn the tables on this foe, though; we can defeat the grave. A victory is possible, however, only through faith in Jesus Christ. With Jesus, we have hope beyond death because we have life.

With Jesus, we win. For all of eternity.

I have always left programs in good shape, and I believe that TCU will be no different.
                                        -- Billy Tubbs as he left TCU

Death is the ultimate opponent;
Jesus is the ultimate victor.

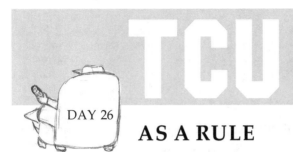

DAY 26

AS A RULE

Read Luke 5:27-32.

"Why do you eat and drink with tax collectors and 'sinners'?" (v. 30b)

Technically, the TCU freshman football team followed the rules and thus secured a victory -- even if it meant having an unconscious player on the field.

In November 1923, the neophyte Frogs had little trouble with Terrel Prep, rolling to a 63-0 win. Only some innovative and downright bizarre finagling, however, kept the rules from handing the win to the high-school team.

As the score mounted, so did TCU's injuries, which was a problem since the team had only twenty players to begin with. Finally, with only about two minutes left in the game, another TCU player hobbled off the field, and when the Frog coach looked around for a healthy substitute, he couldn't find one. He had only ten players able to play.

One of the officials explained that the rules required eleven players on the field. Otherwise, TCU would have to forfeit the game despite the 63-0 score.

Ernest Lowry, who had been badly injured on the opening kickoff and had spent most of the game unconscious on a blanket, managed to get to his feet and declare, "I'm all right, coach. I'll go in." He then promptly passed out again.

That gave the TCU coach an idea, however weird it may have

been. Since TCU was on defense, where that eleventh player was on the field didn't really matter as long as he was back of the line of scrimmage. So, the coach and some players carried Lowry's blanket onto the field just inbounds and placed the unconscious player on it. He was thus, according to the rules, quite legally the eleventh player on the field.

Lowry lay there without moving while the final plays of the game were run and TCU thus claimed its win.

You live by rules that others set up. Some lender determined the interest rate on your mortgage and your car loan. You work hours and shifts somebody else established. Someone else decided what day your garbage gets picked up and what school district your house is in.

Jesus encountered societal rules also, including a strict set of religious edicts that dictated what company he should keep, what people were fit for him to socialize with, to talk to, or to share a meal with. Jesus showed his disdain for the rules by ignoring them. He chose love instead of mindless obedience and demonstrated his contempt for society's rules by mingling with the outcasts, the lowlifes, the poor, and the misfits.

You, too, have to choose when you find yourself in the presence of someone whom society deems undesirable. Will you choose the rules or love? Are you willing to be a rebel for love — as Jesus was for you?

It's the only time an unconscious player ever won a football game.
-- TCU's freshman coach on the 1923 win over Terrel Prep

Society's rules dictate who is and isn't acceptable;
love in Jesus' name knows no such distinctions.

HOW DISAPPOINTING

Read Ezra 3.

*"Many of the older priests and Levites and family heads,
who had seen the former temple, wept aloud when they
saw the foundation of this temple being laid, while many
others shouted for joy" (v. 12).*

Disappointment was the fuel that ignited the greatest season in
TCU's modern football history.

TCU has a long and glittering postseason history, having played
in the second-ever Sugar Bowl in 1935, the first-ever Cotton Bowl
in 1936, and the Orange Bowl in 1941. Not since the 1959 Cotton
Bowl, however, had TCU played in one of the big, prestigious postseason games. What was needed to elevate the Frogs to big-time
status in today's collegiate atmosphere was a win in one of the
Bowl Championship Series bowls.

As the 2009 season progressed and TCU kept winning, a shot
at that goal became a real possibility. When the Frogs finished at
12-0, they were ranked No. 3. They missed out on the BCS Championship Game, but there was no disappointment in playing in the
Fiesta Bowl against 6th-ranked Boise State. The program was
back in the big time.

The disappointment came in the game itself when the Frogs
lost 17-10 to a team they felt they were superior to. In the silence
of a disappointed locker room after the game, head coach Gary
Patterson challenged his players. "I told them, 'You've got to

decide how you will handle this,'" he recalled. "It was like when you're growing up and a kid knocks you down. . . . Are you going to get back up crying, or are you going to get back up, dust yourself off, and move forward from there?"

The Frogs chose to moved forward -- into the legendary 13-0 season of 2010 that was capped by a win in the Rose Bowl.

We know all about disappointment. Friends lie to us or betray us; we lose our jobs through no fault of our own; emotional distance grows between us and our children; the Horned Frogs lose; our dreams shatter.

Disappointment occurs when something or somebody fails to meet the expectations we have for them. Since people are people and can't do anything about that, they inevitably will disappoint us. What is absolutely crucial to our day-to-day living, therefore, is not avoiding disappointment but handling it.

One approach is to act as the old people of Israel did at the dedication of the temple. Instead of joyously celebrating the construction of a new place of worship, they wailed and moaned about the lost glories of the old one. They chose disappointment over lost glories rather than the wonders of the present reality.

Disappointment can paralyze us all, but only if we lose sight of an immutable truth: Our lives may not always be what we wish they were, but God is still good to us.

There's nothing disappointing about Go's love for us.

To us, there was unfinished business.
-- Quarterback Andy Dalton after the loss in the Fiesta Bowl

Even in disappointing times, we can be confident
that God is with us, and therefore life is good.

BE PREPARED

Read Matthew 10:5-23.

"I am sending you out like sheep among wolves. Therefore be as shrewd as snakes and as innocent as doves" (v. 16).

The Frogs faced a daunting challenge when they trotted onto the blue turf of "the toughest place to play in America" -- but they were prepared.

On Nov. 12, 2011, the 7-2 Horned Frogs took on Boise State in Boise. Not only were the Broncos undefeated and ranked fifth in the nation, they had won 35 straight games at home and had not lost a conference game in Boise since 1998. Said one writer, Boise State "didn't lose the game. [TCU head coach Gary] Patterson and the Horned Frogs went into Bronco Stadium and took it." That's because they were prepared; their head coach made sure of it.

The Thursday afternoon before the biggest game of the season, Patterson sat at his desk shuffling papers. "Scouting reports," wrote Gil LeBreton about Patterson's preparation. "Down and distance -- and probably birthdates and shoe sizes." "He was just calm," said linebacker Tank Carder. "He knew all of his players knew what the task at hand was." They were ready.

The game was a classic, and when it came right down to it, Patterson was prepared. Sophomore quarterback Casey Pachall hit freshman receiver Brandon Carter with a touchdown pass with 1:05 on the clock to pull the Frogs to within 35-34. The head Frog then "cement[ed] his Mountain West legacy by brazenly grabbing for it all." He went for two.

After the game, Patterson explained that he went for the win rather than sending the game into overtime "because Boise has so many plays." As prepared as his team and he were, they "surely would have thought of something." But Pachall found Josh Bryce for the 2-point conversion that put the final of 36-35 on the scoreboard and propelled the Frogs to another Mountain West title.

You know the importance of preparation in your own life. You went to the bank for a car loan, facts and figures in hand. That presentation you made at work was seamless because you practiced. The kids' school play suffered no meltdowns because they rehearsed. Knowing what you need to do and doing what you must to succeed isn't luck; it's preparation.

Jesus understood this, and he prepared his followers by lecturing them and by sending them on field trips. Two thousand years later, the life of faith requires similar training and study. You prepare so you'll be ready when that unsaved neighbor standing beside you at your backyard grill asks about Jesus. You prepare so you will know how God wants you to live. You prepare so you are certain in what you believe when the secular, godless world challenges it.

And one day you'll see God face to face. You certainly want to be prepared for that.

That game was won by TCU in the weeks and nights before it.
-- Sportswriter Gil LeBreton on the 2011 Boise State win

**Living in faith requires constant study
and training, preparation for the day
when you meet God face to face.**

YOU NEVER KNOW

Read Acts 26:1-20.

"[I]n all Judea, and to the Gentiles also, I preached that they should repent and turn to God" (v. 20).

Bill Montigel had no idea when he took up golf because he had some time on his hands that he was setting a course for an ultra-successful head-coaching career.

The 2013 season was Montigel's 26th as head men's golf coach at TCU. The team's run to NCAA postseason play was the program's 24th straight, a streak unparalleled in TCU athletic history.

Montigel didn't even play golf when he arrived at TCU; basketball was his sport. He played collegiately at Idaho State for Jim Killingsworth, and when his coach moved to Oklahoma State in 1977, Montigel went with him as a graduate assistant. Killingsworth came to Fort Worth in 1979 to head up the men's basketball program, and Montigel followed him as an assistant coach.

When the NCAA changed its rules about summer recruiting, Montigel and his fellow assistants took up golf to fill up the free time they had, leading Montigel to say over the years that he "stumbled upon" the game. What resulted, though, was an obsession rather than a hobby as he worked to improve his game.

Killingsworth retired at the end of the 1987 season, and Montigel was left without a job. He learned that the men's golf position was open and applied. He had gotten so good as a player that the athletics office had heard of his prowess and decided to hire him. Montigel took the position because he thought it would allow him to play golf every day. He didn't know that most of his time would be taken up by developing one of the most successful programs in collegiate golf.

You never know what you can do until -- like Bill Montigel -- you want to bad enough or until – like Paul -- you have to because God insists. Serving in the military, maybe even in combat. Standing by a friend while everyone else unjustly excoriates her. Undergoing agonizing medical treatment and managing to smile. You never know what life will demand of you.

It's that way too in your relationship with God. As Paul, the most persistent persecutor of the first-century Christians, discovered, you never know what God will ask of you. You can know that God expects you to be faithful; thus, you must be willing to trust him even when he calls you to tasks that appear daunting and beyond your abilities.

You can respond faithfully and confidently to whatever God it is calls you to do for him. That's because even though you never know what lies ahead, you can know with absolutely certainty that God will lead you and will provide what you need. As it was with the Israelites, God will never lead you into the wilderness and then leave you there.

We actually got beat by a team with a basketball coach and no assistant. You've got to be kidding me.
— UCLA golf coach after a loss to TCU by 25 strokes

You never know what God will ask you to do,
but you always know that
he will provide everything you need to do it.

A FAST START

Read Acts 2:40-47.

"Everyone was filled with awe. . . . [They] ate together with glad and sincere hearts, praising God and enjoying the favor of all the people" (vv. 43a, 46b, 47a).

Tossing away the script they had followed to win three straight games, the 1990 Horned Frogs got off to a fast start and proceeded to blow Arkansas out of its own stadium.

After a season-opening loss to Washington State, TCU pulled off three straight fourth-quarter rallies to defeat Missouri, Oklahoma State, and SMU. Concerned about putting themselves in a hole at the start of those games, the players agreed before the contest against 21st-ranked Arkansas that they would take the field with the mind-set that the first quarter was the fourth.

Whatever the players did, it worked. They got off to such a fast start that Arkansas was pretty much whipped by halftime.

Safety Tony Rand started it all when he blocked an Arkansas punt and fell on the ball in the end zone for a touchdown less than two minutes into the game. After Arkansas answered with a field goal, the Frogs drove 79 yards in ten plays for a second first-quarter touchdown. Tight end Kelly Blackwell caught an 18-yard throw from quarterback Leon Clay for the score.

Fourteen points in the first quarter represented a lightning-fast start for the Frogs, but they weren't through. They lit up the scoreboard for 20 points in the second quarter. Two of the scores came less than 90 seconds apart: an 88-yard toss and catch from Clay to flanker Kyle McPherson and another of 57 yards to slotback Richard Woodley.

By halftime, TCU had put 34 points on the board, and the Hogs trailed by 24 points. They just couldn't recover from TCU's fast start. The Frogs finished in their typical strong fashion by scoring two more touchdowns in the fourth quarter, completing a 54-26 rout of the Razorbacks.

Fast starts are crucial for more than football games and races. Any time we begin something new, we want to get out of the gate quickly, jump ahead of the pack, and stay there. We seek to build up momentum from a fast start and keep rolling.

This is true for our faith life also. For a time after we accepted Christ as our savior, we were on fire with a zeal that wouldn't let us rest, much like the early Christians described in Acts. All too many Christians, however, let that blaze die down until only old ashes remain. We become lukewarm pew sitters.

The Christian life shouldn't be that way. Just because we were tepid yesterday doesn't mean we can't be boiling today. Every day we can turn to God for a spiritual tune-up that will put a new spark in our faith life; with a little tending that spark can soon become a raging fire. Today could be the day our faith life gets off to a fast start – again.

Maybe this removes any question about whether our last three comeback wins were flukes.
-- Tight end Kelly Blackwell on the fast start and rout vs. Arkansas

**Every day offers us yet another chance
to get off to a fast start for Jesus.**

BLESS YOU

Read Romans 5:1-11.

"We also rejoice in our sufferings because we know that suffering produces perseverance; perseverance, character; and character, hope. And hope does not disappoint us" (vv. 3-5a).

An injury that required surgery and sidelined him for a year turned into one of the greatest blessings of Matt Carpenter's life.

Carpenter started in the Frog infield as a freshmen and a sophomore in 2005 and '06. His sophomore season he was second on the team with a .349 average. He was ready, therefore, for a great season in 2007.

Before he suited up for his first game, though, Carpenter felt a nagging pain in his right elbow. It got so bad he couldn't make the throw to first base from third base; head coach Jim Schlossnagle protected him by moving him to first. He also lost some of the pop from his bat. "It got to where I couldn't even sleep. I was in too much pain," Carpenter said.

In the seventh game of the season, Carpenter told his coach to take him out; he couldn't play. Two days later, a doctor diagnosed a torn ligament that required Tommy John surgery to repair. Carpenter would miss the rest of the season. Thus began what Schlossnagle called "a reawakening" for Carpenter's life.

With time for some harsh self-evaluation, Carpenter realized he had not taken care of himself. "I felt like I was a bit out of shape last year," he said. He shed 50 pounds, replacing bulk with strength and agility. He consulted a sports psychologist to help prepare him for his comeback from the injury.

His baseball career rejuvenated, Carpenter started every game in 2008 and '09, hitting .333 his senior season. He set a new TCU single-season record for doubles in '09 and finished second all--time in hits, doubles, and walks. The blessing disguised as an injury spurred him all the way to a major-league career with the St. Louis Cardinals.

We just never know what God is up to. We can know, though, that he's always busy preparing blessings for us and that if we trust and obey him, he will pour out those blessings upon us.

Some of those blessings, however, come disguised as hardship and suffering as was the case with Matt Carpenter. That's often true in our own lives, too, and it is only after we can look back upon what we have endured that we understand it as a blessing.

The key lies in trusting God, in realizing that God isn't out to destroy us but instead is interested only in doing good for us, even if that means allowing us to endure the consequences of a difficult lesson. God doesn't manage a candy store; more often, he relates to us as a stern, but always loving, father. If we truly love and trust God, no matter what our situation is now, he has blessings in store for us. This, above all, is our greatest hope.

My dad told me everything happens for a reason and God has a plan for me. He told me to look on the bright side.
-- Matt Carpenter on the injury that turned into a blessing

Life's hardships are often transformed into blessings when we endure them trusting in God.

DAY 32

STRANGE BUT TRUE

Read Isaiah 55.

"My thoughts are not your thoughts, neither are your ways my way" (v. 8).

Strange but true: TCU recruited one of the greatest players in college and pro football history primarily as a baseball player.

From 1934-36, Sammy Baugh quarterbacked the Frogs to 29 wins, the most until Andy Dalton broke the record. (See Devotion No. 2.) He was a two-time All-America who led TCU to 12 wins and the national title in 1935. He was a charter member of the Pro Football Hall of Fame (1963) and was inducted into the College Football Hall of Fame in 1951. TCU's indoor practice facility is named in Baugh's honor.

Baugh played end through junior high. Before his family moved to Sweetwater, his high school team in Temple "couldn't beat anyone." One day his head coach told him, "We can't run on anybody and we can't stop anybody. Maybe we can throw on 'em. I'm putting you in at tailback (the single-wing equivalent of quarterback)." The man who would be called "college football's greatest passer" gained his proficiency by practicing endlessly at throwing a football through a swinging tire, often on the run.

His first love, however, was baseball, and Baugh was actually viewed as a better baseball prospect coming out of high school. He was recruited to TCU by Dutch Meyer, the baseball coach. Meyer recruited Baugh as a baseball player with the understanding that

66   DAY 32

he could also play football. Then, in one of life's strange quirks, in 1934 when Baugh was a sophomore, Meyer was named the head football coach.

Baugh did play third base for TCU and was good enough to sign a contract with the St. Louis Cardinals out of college. Strangely enough, a Texas sportswriter dubbed him "Slingin' Sammy" for his exploits on the diamond and not the gridiron.

Some things in life are so strange their existence can't really be explained. How else can we account for the popularity of the Kardashians, tattoos, curling, tofu, and the behavior of teenagers?

And how strange is God's plan to save us? Think a minute about what God did. He could have come roaring down, destroying and blasting everyone whose sinfulness offended him, which, of course, is pretty much all of us. Then he could have brushed off his hands, nodded the divine head, and left a scorched planet in his wake. All in a day's work.

Instead, God came up with a totally novel plan: He would save the world by becoming a human being, letting himself be humiliated, tortured, and killed, thus establishing a kingdom of justice and righteousness that will last forever.

It's a strange way to save the world, and we probably wouldn't have ever even considered such a radical idea -- but thanks be to God his ways are not our ways.

Dutch [Meyer] recruited me for baseball with the idea that I could also play football.
— Sammy Baugh

It's strange but true: God allowed himself to be killed on a cross to save the world.

LIMITED-TIME OFFER

Read Psalm 103.

*"As for man, his days are like grass, he flourishes like a
flower of the field; the wind blows over it and it is gone.
. . . But from everlasting to everlasting the Lord's love is
with those who fear him" (vv. 15-17).*

During a TCU football game in 1971, something unimaginable
happened: The head coach collapsed and died.

After a stint as the head man at Tulane, Jim Pittman took over
the TCU program in 1971, succeeding Fred Taylor. His Frogs beat
Texas-Arlington 42-0 in his first game, and the team was 2-3-1
when it took on Baylor in Waco on Oct. 30.

Early in the first quarter, Pittman collapsed and was taken to
a hospital where he was pronounced dead of an apparent heart
attack. After only ten months on the job, he was gone.

At halftime, the coaches told the players of their coach's death
though some had heard of it from a policemen on the sideline
before the first half ended. "He was just a great leader and a great
man," said TCU quarterback Steve Judy. Bill Tohill, Pittman's chief
aide and longtime friend, said that in the shocked and emotional
locker room, "We made a promise to win [the] game for him."

Early in the third quarter, it looked as though the players were
too distracted by Pittman's death to play much decent football.
Baylor nabbed an interception and then went the distance on
the first play to lead 27-20. Somehow, however, the Frogs held

themselves together and made good on their promise.

They answered Baylor's score with a 75-yard drive. Steve Patterson and Lane Bowen chewed up most of the yardage with Judy scoring from the 5. Berl Simmons' PAT tied the game.

The teams swapped punts for a while until TCU mounted the game-winning drive. On third down from the Baylor 10, Judy hit Ronnie Peoples with a strike, and the All-SWC end carried two defenders with him across the goal line. Simmons' kick put the final score of 34-27 on the board with ten minutes left.

The Horned Frogs had won one for their coach.

A heart attack, cancer, or an accident will probably take -- or has already taken -- someone you know or love who is "too young to die," someone such as Jim Pittman, who was only 46.

The death of a younger person never seems to "make sense." That's because such a death belies the common view of death as the natural end of a life lived well and lived long. Moreover, you can't see the whole picture as God does, so you can't know how the death furthers God's kingdom.

At such a time, you can seize the comforting truth that God is in control and therefore everything will be all right one day. You can also gain a sense of urgency in your own life by appreciating that God's offer of life through Jesus Christ is a limited-time offer that expires at your death – and there's no guarantee about when that will be.

We wanted to win it for [Jim Pittman] and in his memory.
-- TCU assistant coach Russell Coffee on the '71 Baylor game

**God offers you life through Jesus Christ,
but you must accept the offer before your death.**

CELEBRATION TIME

Read Luke 15:1-10.

"There is rejoicing in the presence of the angels of God over one sinner who repents" (v. 10).

For Harry Moreland, the celebration of his game-winning score was tougher than the game.

One day after a snowstorm, TCU met Texas on Nov. 14, 1959, in Memorial Stadium. The game was a showdown, although the Longhorns were expected to provide most of the show. They were 8-0 and ranked No. 2 in the country. The Frogs were the defending Southwest Conference champions, but they went into the game at 5-2. One newspaper headline that week declared, "Defending Champion Meets Heir Apparent."

The first half went the way everybody expected with Texas leading 9-0. The last thirty minutes belonged to TCU. The defense, led by end Don Floyd and tackle Bob Lilly, both All-Americas, held Texas to one first down and 21 total yards the last half. That gave the offense, led by All-American fullback Jack Spikes, room and time to score a touchdown that cut the Longhorn lead to 9-7.

In the fourth quarter, Moreland, a fleet 170-lb. junior halfback, slid through a hole created by the right side of the line, juked the first defensive back with a shot at him, and then outran the rest of the Texas defenders for a 56-yard sprint.

In the end zone, a jubilant Moreland jumped up and down until he was "enthusiastically pummeled by his teammates." That celebration led Moreland to declare, "I haven't been hit this hard all year."

Moreland's run put the final of 14-9 on the scoreboard in an upset that the Frogs dominated, outgaining Texas 233 yards to 97. TCU went on to more celebrations that season, finishing 8-2 with a ranking in the top 10 and tying Texas and Arkansas for the SWC championship.

TCU just whipped Texas. You got that new job or that promotion. You just held your newborn child in your arms. Life has those grand moments that call for celebration. You may jump up and down and scream in a wild frenzy at Amon G. Carter Stadium or share a quiet, sedate candlelight dinner for two at home -- but you celebrate.

Consider then a celebration that is beyond our imagining, one that fills every niche and corner of the very home of God and the angels. Imagine a celebration in Heaven, which also has its grand moments.

Those grand moments are touched off when someone comes to faith in Jesus. Heaven itself rings with the joyous sounds of the singing and dancing of the celebrating angels. Even God rejoices when just one person – you or someone you have introduced to Christ -- turns to him.

When you said "yes" to Christ, you made the angels dance.

When it comes to celebrating, act like you've been there before.
-- College football coach Terry Bowden

**God himself joins the angels in heavenly
celebration when even a single person
turns to him through faith in Jesus.**

CHANGE YOUR TUNE

Read Romans 6:1-14.

"Just as Christ was raised from the dead through the glory of the Father, we too may live a new life" (v. 4).

After more than a year on the road, Katariina Tuohimaa was ready for a change. That meant TCU.

Tuohimaa had her life all mapped out as a high school senior in Finland in 2006. She was a tennis phenom, and she planned to play professional tennis. "I'm not applying to study anywhere," she said in a newspaper interview. "I'm ready for the nomadic life on the road."

So she took off, starting far outside the top 100 in the women's rankings. All the while, she ducked calls and e-mails from TCU tennis coach Jeff Hammond. A foot fracture slowed her down, and after more than a year on the road with the 24/7 grind of pro tennis, Tuohimaa found herself in a hotel room in Mexico questioning what she was doing. "I was traveling alone and couldn't go anywhere," she said. "I really wanted to play tennis, but was there anything else?"

She decided the answer was yes. That anything else was Hammond and TCU, and she was ready for a change. So she got in touch with the persistent coach. In late 2007, she gave Hammond the okay to sign her to a tennis scholarship.

Rushing against deadlines all the way, Tuohimaa took the SAT and obtained a student visa. She entered TCU in time for the 2008 season and made an immediate impact, pairing with sophomore Kayla Duncan as the squad's top doubles team.

Tuohimaa was All-Mountain West in both singles and doubles all four seasons at TCU. She was also named to the Mountain West All-Academic Team each of her four seasons. She finished her college career in 2011, declaring that "giving into Hammond's overtures was the best decision she ever made."

Even if it meant radically changing her life.

Anyone who asserts no change is needed in his or her life just isn't paying attention. Every life has doubt, worry, fear, failure, frustration, unfulfilled dreams, and unsuccessful relationships in some combination. The memory and consequences of our past often haunt and trouble us.

Simply recognizing the need for change in our lives, though, doesn't mean the changes that will bring about hope, joy, peace, and fulfillment will occur. We need some power greater than ourselves or we wouldn't be where we are.

So where can we turn to? Where lies the hope for a changed life? It lies in an encounter with the Lord of all Hope: Jesus Christ. For a life turned over to Jesus, change is inevitable. With Jesus in charge, the old self with its painful and destructive ways of thinking, feeling, loving, and living is transformed.

A changed life is always only a talk with Jesus away.

I chased her for two years. She knew about us, but she hadn't changed her mind [about pro tennis] until she got hold of us.
-- TCU coach Jeff Hammond on Katariina Tuohimaa

**In Jesus lie the hope and the power
that change lives.**

DAY 36

JUST PERFECT

Read Matthew 5:43-48.

"Be perfect, therefore, as your heavenly Father is perfect"
(v. 48).

In 2010, the Horned Frogs achieved the goal of every football team every season: perfection.

Since college football became recognizable as the sport we see today, the Frogs had achieved perfection only in 1938. Two other teams -- 1929 and 1932 -- were undefeated but tied. Then along came 2010 with its 13-0 perfection.

It was no fluke. While Ohio State's president chided TCU for not playing the "murderer's row" schedule of the Big Ten conference, the Frogs made a mockery of his comments by ending the season with a 21-19 win over Wisconsin of the Big Ten in the Rose Bowl. The team could only play the schedule it was dealt, and perfection was the result.

The Frogs had the top-ranked defense in the country, a unit that held seven of its twelve opponents to single digits, a remarkable feat in an age of wide-open offenses and high-scoring games. Linebacker Tank Carder, safety Tejay Johnson, and defensive end Wayne Daniels were All-Americas.

Signaling to the world that they were ready to take the step up in competition that they made in 2012 with the move to the Big 12, the Frogs dominated their fellow Mountain West compatriots. TCU buried the heart of its conference schedule -- BYU, Air Force, and Utah -- by a combined score of 116-17. The only league team to play the Frogs close was San Diego State, which scored two fourth-quarter touchdowns to make the final a deceptive 40-35.

The season wasn't perfect, however, until Carder knocked down a Badger pass on a 2-point conversion try with exactly two minutes left to play. "13-0 is top of the mountain," head coach Gary Patterson said after game. And it was perfection.

As individuals, we are not perfect; we make mistakes every day. We botch our personal relationships; at work we seek competence, not perfection. To insist upon personal or professional perfection in our lives is to establish an impossibly high standard that will eventually destroy us physically, emotionally, and mentally.

Yet that is exactly the standard God sets for us. Our love is to be perfect, never ceasing, never failing, never qualified – just the way God loves us. And Jesus didn't limit his command to only preachers and goody-two-shoes types. All of his disciples are to be perfect as they navigate their way through the world's ambiguous definition and understanding of love.

But that's impossible! Well, not necessarily, if to love perfectly is to serve God wholeheartedly and to follow Jesus with single-minded devotion. Anyhow, in his perfect love for us, God makes allowance for our imperfect love and the consequences of it in the perfection of Jesus.

The memories will be forever.
-- Writer Gil LeBreton on the perfect season of 2010

In his perfect love for us, God provides a way
for us to escape the consequences
of our imperfect love for him: Jesus.

MEMORY LOSS

Read 1 Corinthians 11:17-29.

"[D]o this in remembrance of me" (v. 24).

More than sixty years after it happened, Johnny Vaught still remembered the hit.

Vaught is best remembered for his hall-of-fame coaching career at Ole Miss where he won 190 games and six SEC titles. Before he was a coach, though, Vaught was an All-American guard at TCU.

On Nov. 11, 1932, the undefeated Frogs hosted the once-beaten Texas Longhorns in a showdown for the Southwest Conference title. On the field that day was an astounding array of talent. On one side was the TCU line of ends Dan Salkeld and Madison Pruitt, tackles Foster Howell and Ben Boswell, guards Vaught and Lon Evans, and center J.W. Townsend. They played both ways, and six of the seven were chosen All-SWC. Salkeld was the only one not to make it, and he missed part of the season with an injury.

On the other side of the line was the Texas backfield with three of the four all-conference players. Actually, ten of the eleven All-SWC players played that day since TCU's Blanard Spearman was the fourth back.

The Frogs won 14-0 on their way to a 10-0-1 season. For a while, Vaught wasn't sure that he would be around at the finish -- because of the hit. He released early to cover punts. As Vaught recalled it, on one punt, "I went down there and the return man suddenly veered . . . and I swerved to meet him." And that's when it happened. The other return man hit Vaught "about as hard as you can hit somebody. Knocked me clear across the field."

Vaught said he wasn't really hurt by the blow, "but it knocked the breath out of me and I couldn't talk." The Frogs called time out since rules required that a player who came out of the game couldn't go back in until the next quarter.

Vaught recovered and played on, but he never forgot the hit.

Memory makes us who we are. Whether our memories appear as pleasant reverie or unnerving nightmares, they shape us and to a large extent determine both our actions and our reactions. Alzheimer's is so terrifying because it steals our memory from us, and in the process we lose ourselves. We disappear.

The greatest tragedy of our lives is that God remembers. In response to that photographic memory, he condemns us for our sin. Paradoxically, the greatest joy of our lives is that God remembers. In response to that memory, he came as Jesus to wash even the memory of our sins away.

God uses memory as a tool through which we encounter revival. At the Last Supper, Jesus instructed his disciples and us to remember. In sharing this unique meal with fellow believers and remembering Jesus and his actions, we meet Christ again, not just as a memory but as an actual living presence.

To remember is to keep our faith alive.

[The] hit [on Johnny Vaught] became one of those legendary moments that was still [remembered] 30 years later.
-- Writer Whit Canning

Because we remember Jesus,
God will not remember our sins.

TEAM PLAYERS

Read 1 Corinthians 12:4-13, 27-31.

"Now to each one the manifestation of the Spirit is given for the common good" (v. 7).

All of TCU's athletic programs are team sports, but only one involves team members with four legs.

TCU's varsity equestrian program was launched in 2007 and immediately became one of the school's most successful teams. In only their second season of competition, the equestrians won a national championship. The Frogs thereby became the fastest team to win a title in the sport's history. The national championship was TCU's first since the women's golf team claimed an NCAA title in 1983.

The sport is certainly unusual since half the team members are horses. That in itself makes it perhaps the most unpredictable of all collegiate sports because the horses inevitably arrive with minds and attitudes of their own. TCU rider Courtney Motz illustrated the problem when she said she never knew how a horse would react at any moment. She thus expected each ride to be different from all her previous rides.

To prepare for the different personalities of their four-legged teammates, TCU's two-legged riders switch horses each day at practice, as per coach Logan Fiorentino's directions. This works quite well at home since the home team furnishes the horses, but the equines don't travel to road meets. Each rider thus has only about four minutes to familiarize herself with her four-legged teammate for a day before competition begins.

TCU rider Haley Jacobi, a senior in 2012-13, said she bonds with the horses she rides, just as she would any other teammate. "You can feel when the horses are tense and nervous or when they are completely willing and relaxed," she said. For Jacobi, Overtime, her favorite horse, was "a Frog for life, definitely a team leader."

Most accomplishments are the result of teamwork, whether it's a college sports team, the running of a household, the completion of a project at work, or a dance recital. Disparate talents and gifts work together for the common good and the greater goal.

A church works exactly the same way. At its most basic, a church is a team that has been and is being assembled by God. A shared faith drives the team members and impels them toward shared goals. As a successful equestrian team must have capable riders and trained horses, so must a church be composed of people with different spiritual and personal gifts. The result is something greater than everyone involved.

What makes a church team different from others is that the individual efforts are expended for the glory of God and not self. The nature of a church member's particular talents doesn't matter; what does matter is that those talents are used as part of God's team.

They're teammates, not just horses.

– TCU equestrian Kaitlin Perry

A church is a team of people using their various talents and gifts for God, the source of all those abilities.

A HELPING HAND

Read Psalm 121.

"My help comes from the Lord, the maker of heaven and earth" (v. 2).

Isabel Petta had no idea who the handsome stranger was that stopped to help her out, but her husband, Chris, sure knew him.

On Labor Day 2009, Petta was engaged in a familiar routine -- a nine-mile walk -- as she was preparing for the Dallas/Fort Worth Breast Cancer 3-Day, a 60-mile walk in November. As usual, her 50-lb. collie-shepherd mix, Buddy, was with her.

This day, though, suddenly turned into anything but the usual because Buddy didn't finish the walk. He collapsed near the TCU campus and lay on his side, panting and foaming at the mouth. "I was distraught. I didn't know what to do," Petta said.

She used her cellphone to call her husband for help but didn't get an answer. Desperate, she flagged down an SUV driven by a young man. She told him of her plight, and he drove Petta to her car a few blocks away. Then to her surprise, he followed her back to where Buddy lay, still in distress. He had some water in his SUV, and he got out and gave the dog a drink. He then helped Petta get Buddy into her car.

Back home, Buddy enjoyed a short rest and soon was up and around, recovered completely from his bout with the heat. Petta related her adventure to her husband, emphasizing the help she had received from the nice, kind young person.

HORNED FROGS

"What was his name?" Chris asked. "Andy," she replied. That piqued the hubby's interest. "Andy who?" he asked. "Andy Dalton," an unaware Isabel answered. Chris had one more question for his wife: "Did he have red hair?" "Yes," Isabel said.

Her good Samaritan and Buddy's buddy was the All-American starting quarterback for the Horned Frogs and perhaps the most famous player of the modern TCU era.

In any tightly contested game no matter what the sport, the Horned Frogs have their ups and downs. So do we in our daily lives. Sometimes – often more than once in the journey that is our life – we get to a point when our own resources won't get us through. We need help.

But where to turn? Family and friends? Counselors? A pastor? They're certainly better options than the likes of drugs or alcohol. But people are fallible, and thus they sometimes let us down even when they try their best. They simply, for whatever reason, can't or won't always provide what we need.

They're derivative anyway; that is, they were all created. The answer for meaningful, life-changing help that will never fail is the Source – Almighty God. God cares for his people, each one of us. The creator of the cosmos cares about you. He knows you by name and knows exactly what's going on in your life. And he has the power and the desire to help – as no one or nothing else can.

Once I leave this earth, I know I've done something that will continue to help others.

-- Jackie Joyner-Kersee

"May I help you?" isn't just for a store;
it's a question God will ask if you turn to him.

TOLD YOU SO

Read Matthew 24:15-31.

"See, I have told you ahead of time" (v. 25).

They said Blaize Foltz was too small, that he couldn't cut it. He showed them all.

Young Blaize received some glances from Big-12 recruiters when he was in high school because his dad, Roger, was his coach. "They'd stop by the school . . . to glad-hand and say how much they liked the highlight reel [Roger had] sent of Blaize bulldozing kids." Then they'd take one look at him on the practice field and deliver their ultimatum about big-time college football: "Too small." Young Foltz just wasn't the behemoth the Big 12 required its offensive linemen to be.

A former offensive lineman himself, Roger told his son, "You are a great player. We're gonna keep working."

And so they did. In addition to the weight room, the physical training, and the o-line fundamentals he passed on from his own experience, Foltz Senior implemented a regimented, high-protein diet for his son. He kept turkey sandwiches in the faculty lounge and used the blender there to mix shakes. At 2 a.m. each day, young Foltz awoke to wolf down a peanut butter sandwich. The result was 100 pounds and the high school's first-ever Division I scholarship athlete. Blaize Foltz came to TCU.

He started some as a freshman in 2009; an injury shortened his sophomore season. Then Foltz came into his own his junior season, earning All-Mountain West honors at right guard. As a senior in 2012, he was 6'4" tall and weighed 310 pounds. He was a leader in the weight room who had to eat fish and give up Whataburgers and Dr. Pepper to keep his weight down.

When TCU moved into the Big 12 in 2012, the significance was not lost on the Foltz men. Blaize was All-Big 12 Second Team and an honorable mention selection for Big 12 Offensive Lineman of the Year. He could truly look at all those Big-12 coaches who had disparaged him and tell them, "I told you so."

Don't you just hate it in when somebody says, "I told you so"? That means the other person was right and you were wrong; that other person has spoken the truth. You could have listened to that know-it-all in the first place, but then you would have lost the chance yourself to crow, "I told you so."

In our pluralistic age and society, many view truth as relative, meaning absolute truth does not exist and therefore all belief systems have equal value and merit. But this is a ghastly, dangerous fallacy because it ignores the truth that God proclaimed in the presence and words of Jesus.

In speaking the truth, Jesus told everybody exactly what he was going to do: come back and take his faithful followers with him. Those who don't listen or who don't believe will be left behind with those four awful words, "I told you so," ringing in their ears and wringing their souls.

A lot of people told me I can't do stuff. I just kind of use it as my fuel.
-- Blaize Foltz

Jesus matter-of-factly told us what he has planned:
He will return to gather all the faithful to himself.

CLOTHES HORSE

Read Genesis 37:1-11.

"Israel loved Joseph more than all his children, because he was the son of his old age: and he made him a coat of many colours" (v. 3 KJV).

For Brent Hackett, it was really all about the shoes.

A 6-2 guard, Hackett finished his TCU career with the 2007-08 season after which he received honorable mention All-Mountain West laurels for the second straight season. He scored 1,103 points in his career, 18th in school history.

At TCU, Hackett also gained considerable fame off the court, not for something he did, but for something he had: shoes. His collection of basketball sneakers was so large -- more than 300 pairs, according to him -- that he called himself a "shoehead." After all, he had more basketball shoes than all his teammates and coaches combined.

To use the old-fashioned term "sneakers" to refer to Hackett's collection of footwear is, in truth, incorrect. His shoes are anything but out of date. Air Force Ones, Air Assaults, Air Dunks, Air Zoom BBs -- he had them all when he was at TCU.

His obsession with shoes frequently provided Hackett with the chance to show a rather startling mnemonic ability. He could recite from memory the release dates and model numbers of each pair of his shoes. As head coach Neil Dougherty put it, "He's our resident expert. All the players ask his advice on what to buy and where to find the best deals."

Hackett was the team captain his senior season as he averaged 11.6 points per game, the best of his career. Throughout his time in Fort Worth, though, he was hampered by nagging injuries to both shoulders and to his left knee. As he prepared for his senior season, he switched his jersey number to change his luck -- but he kept the shoes.

Contemporary society proclaims that it's all about the clothes. Buy that new suit or dress, those new shoes, and all the sparkling accessories, and you'll be a new person.

It's just advertising hyperbole, though, because any changes clothes make in us are only cosmetic; underneath, we're still the same persons. Consider Joseph, for instance, prancing about in his pretty new clothes; he was still a spoiled little tattletale whom his brothers detested enough to sell into slavery.

Jesus never taught that we should run around half-naked or wear only second-hand clothes from the local mission. He did warn us, though, against making consumer items such as clothes a priority in our lives. A follower of Christ seeks to emulate Jesus not through material, superficial means such as wearing special clothing like a robe and sandals.

Rather, the disciple desires to match Jesus' inner beauty and serenity -- whether the clothes the Christian wears are the sables of a king or the rags of a pauper.

Definitely more [shoes] than I have matching clothes to go with them.
-- Brent Hackett on the extent of his footwear collection

**Where Jesus is concerned, clothes
don't make the person; faith does.**

A GOOD IMPRESSION

Read John 1:1-18.

"In the beginning was the Word, and the Word was with God, and the Word was God. . . . The Word became flesh and made his dwelling among us" (vv. 1, 14).

They were being scrutinized by representatives from three of the BCS bowls, so the Horned Frogs needed to make a good impression. Boy, did they ever.

On Nov. 14, 2009, the undefeated and 4th-ranked Frogs hosted the 16th-ranked Utes from Utah. With a 9-0 record, TCU clearly had its sights on crashing the private party that was the BCS. Since they were in the Mountain West Conference and didn't have an automatic berth in one of the big bowls if they won the league title, the Frogs needed to be impressive against a good Utah team.

The TCU fan base knew how important the game was, showing up in record numbers for the showdown. Along with representatives from the Orange, Rose, and Fiesta bowls, they walked away impressed by what they saw. In fact, they stormed the field when the game was over. Or at least when the clock ran down. The game was over long before the time ran out.

In one of the most impressive showings in TCU history, the Frogs scored three touchdowns in less than three minutes of the second quarter and went on to slaughter the Utes 55-28, upping their win streak to twelve.

Six different Frogs made it into the end zone. Ed Wesley ran for

HORNED FROGS

137 yards and a touchdown, and Andy Dalton threw for 207 yards, including a TD pass to senior Ryan Christian. Matthew Tucker scored the first and last touchdowns on runs of 41 and 9 yards.

Early in the second quarter, Jeremy Kerley scored from the 1 and then had a 39-yard punt return that set up Antoine Hicks' TD run. When Tank Carder returned an interception 15 yards for a touchdown, TCU led 35-7 with 11:40 to go -- in the first half.

The Horned Frogs were -- to say the least -- quite impressive.

That guy in the apartment next door. A job search complete with interview. A twenty-year class reunion. The new neighbors. Like the TCU football team, we are constantly about the fraught task of wanting to make an impression on people. We want them to remember us, obviously in a flattering way.

We make that impression, good or bad, generally in two ways. Even with instant communication on the Internet – perhaps especially with the Internet – we primarily influence the opinion others have of us by our words. After that, we can advance to the next level by making an impression with our actions.

God gave us an impression of himself in exactly the same way. In Jesus, God took the unprecedented step of appearing to mortals as one of us, as mere flesh and bone. We now know for all time the sorts of things God does and the sorts of things God says. In Jesus, God put his divine foot forward to make a good impression on each one of us.

The Frogs put on quite a show.
-- CSTV.com writer on the impression TCU made vs. the Utes

Through Jesus' words and actions,
God seeks to impress us with his love.

DAY 43

THE FAME GAME

Read 1 Kings 10:1-10, 18-29.

*"King Solomon was greater in riches and wisdom than
all the other kings of the earth. The whole world sought
audience with Solomon" (vv. 23-24).*

Sammy Baugh remains a football legend to this day, but for a
brief time, he found fame as a Hollywood cowboy.

Following his stellar collegiate career at TCU, Baugh turned
pro and was an immediate sensation, leading the Washington
Redskins to the league championship in 1937, his rookie season.
After the 1940 season, to his surprise, someone from Republic
Pictures called him at home and said they wanted him to make a
movie. Baugh flew out to Hollywood without an agent or a lawyer
and signed a contract for $4,500.

The movie turned out to be a 12-part Saturday matinee serial
called *King of the Texas Rangers*. During his six weeks on the set,
Baugh rubbed elbows with some famous people such as Duncan
Renaldo, who played the Cisco Kid, stuntman Tom Steele, and
Pauline Moore, who made movies with the likes of Henry Fonda
and Roy Rogers.

Years later, Baugh recalled that the first day on the set the
director gave him some paper and told him they were lines for
the next day and he had to study them. This went on for three
days with Baugh dutifully studying lines that were never used.
When he told Renaldo about it, the star laughed and advised him

to forget about the lines. "They'll tell you what to say."

Baugh did most of his own stunts and much of his riding. He rode one horse who was so perfectly trained for the movies that "the minute somebody hollered 'Action!' that old blaze was long gone -- whether I was ready or not."

After his brush with Hollywood fame, Baugh headed back east for more gridiron fame with the Redskins.

Have you ever wanted to be famous? Hanging out with other rich and famous people, having folks with microphones listen to what you say, throwing money around, meeting adoring and clamoring fans, signing autographs, and posing for photographs?

Many of us yearn to be famous, well-known in the places and by the people that we believe matter. That's all fame amounts to: strangers knowing your name and your face.

The truth is that you are already famous where it really does matter, which excludes TV's talking heads, screaming teenagers, rapt moviegoers, or D.C. power brokers. You are famous because Almighty God knows your name, your face, and everything else there is to know about you.

If a persistent photographer snapped you pondering this fame – the only kind that has eternal significance – would the picture show the world unbridled joy or the shell-shocked expression of a mug shot?

I can recall no other six-week period in my life that I so thoroughly enjoyed as the time I spent on that picture.
– Sammy Baugh on his fling as a Hollywood movie star

You're already famous because
God knows your name and your face,
which may be either reassuring or terrifying.

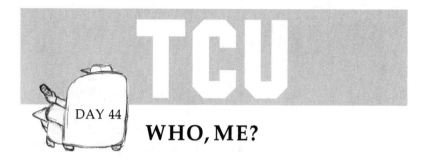

DAY 44

WHO, ME?

Read Judges 6:11-23.

"'But Lord,' Gideon asked, 'how can I save Israel? My clan is the weakest in Manasseh, and I am the least in my family'" (v. 15).

Leon Clay was just minding his own business when suddenly the head coach bellowed his name.

In September and October of 1989, Clay, a redshirt freshman, spent most of his Saturday afternoons on the sideline watching starter Ron Jiles lead the offense. "No hits, no long runs, no errors, no bruises." Through the first six games of life as the team's No.-2 quarterback, he had tried three passes and completed one and had run the ball six times for 28 yards. He was "a player whose feet were not even damp, much less wet." Clay's time would come, but not this season.

With 19th-ranked Air Force in the house on Oct. 21, Clay expected another day when pregame warm ups would provide his most strenuous activity. Suddenly, though, his peaceful, calm, and relaxed afternoon ended with 1:03 left in the first quarter when head coach Jim Wacker shouted, "Leon!" It sounded like what it was: a frantic SOS call. Jiles had come off the field nursing his right wrist.

Clay's reaction was immediate: "A bunch of butterflies suddenly took flight in his stomach." The head Frog recalled that Clay's surprise and nervousness showed. "He had a big frown,"

HORNED FROGS

Wacker said. "I told him to show me a big smile and go out there and have some fun. I had to tell him again, but then his face really lit up."

So did Clay's game. After his initial surprise at being called on, he came through for the Frogs. He hit 10 of 11 passes for 165 yards and two touchdowns and quarterbacked TCU to a 27-9 upset.

As sportswriter Galen Wilkins put it, "[Leon] Clay never knew he'd sweat out a uniform [against Air Force]. He must know now, though, that it looked good on him."

You probably know exactly how Leon Clay felt; you've experienced that moment of unwelcome surprise with its sinking "who, me?" feeling. How about that time the teacher called on you when you hadn't done a lick of homework? Or the night the hypnotist pulled you out of a room full of folks to be his guinea pig? You've had the wide-eyed look and the turmoil in your midsection when you were suddenly singled out and found yourself in a situation you neither sought nor were prepared for.

You may feel exactly as Gideon did about being called to serve God in some way, quailing at the very notion of being audacious enough to teach Sunday school, coordinate a high school prayer club, or lead a small group study. Who, me? Hey, who's worthy enough to do anything like that?

The truth is that nobody is – but that doesn't seem to matter to God. And it's his opinion, not yours, that counts.

Big butterflies. The biggest I've felt since my first game in high school.
-- Leon Clay on what he felt when Jim Wacker called his name

You're right in that no one is worthy to serve God,
but the problem is that doesn't matter to God.

PRAYER WARRIORS

Read Luke 18:1-8.

"Then Jesus told his disciples a parable to show them that they should always pray and not give up" (v. 1).

Marcus Cannon and his family knew exactly what to do when he was diagnosed with cancer: pray.

From 2007-2010, Cannon was a fixture on the Frogs' offensive line. After playing at right tackle in all thirteen games as a redshirt freshman, he was a starter in 2008 and was Honorable Mention All-Mountain West Conference. In 2009, he did not give up a single sack and was first-team all-conference. Moved to left tackle for his senior season of 2010, he was again all-conference and received some All-America honors. All the while, though, Cannon's body, which grew to 6'6" and 350 lbs., carried a secret.

When Cannon was 15, he discovered a lump in his lower abdomen that doctors diagnosed as an infection. It didn't go away, and during his redshirt sophomore season at TCU, he had a needle biopsy. "They always told me it was OK," he said. With the 2011 NFL draft pending, Cannon had a full biopsy. Eight days before the draft, he learned he had cancer of the lymphatic system.

"With tears in his eyes and death in his thoughts, [Cannon] drove his Toyota truck five hours to his parents' house." As he drove, he not only cried, he prayed. When he broke the news, the family responded immediately; they gathered to pray. "We are a religious family, and we know prayer changes things," said

Marcus' father. "That was pretty much all I knew to do given the situation we were facing."

Bolstered by ongoing prayer, Cannon had his initial chemo treatment on the first day of the draft. In July, he finished his chemo and reported to the Patriots in August. He played in seven games in 2011, all sixteen games in 2012, and then was moved to right guard prior to the 2013 season.

"I have a will," Cannon said. And he had prayer. As Jesus taught us to do, Marcus Cannon prayed and didn't give up.

Any problems we may have with prayer and its results derive from our side, not God's. We pray for a while about something – perhaps fervently at first – but our enthusiasm wanes if we don't receive the answer we want exactly when we want it. Why waste our time by asking for the same thing over and over again?

But God isn't deaf; God does hear our prayers, and God does respond to them. As Jesus clearly taught, our prayers have an impact because they turn the power of Almighty God loose in this world. Thus, falling to our knees and praying to God is not a sign of weakness and helplessness. Rather, praying for someone or something is an aggressive act, an intentional ministry, a conscious and fervent attempt on our part to change someone's life or the world for the better.

God responds to our prayers; we often just can't perceive or understand how he is working to make those prayers come about.

All I can do is keep doing what I'm doing. That's to keep praying and accept my healing.

-- *Marcus Cannon*

Jesus told us to always pray and never give up.

DAY 46

KEEP OUT!

Read Exodus 26:31-35; 30:1-10.

"The curtain will separate the Holy Place from the Most Holy Place" (v. 26:33).

The TCU baseball team was kicked out of its own locker room and its own playing field. The result was school history.

As head coach Jim Schlossnagle saw it, success had gone to the Horned Frogs' collective heads. 2009 had been a great season. TCU won 40 games, including a 3-0 sweep of a regional, and came within one win of the College World Series for the first time in school history. That marked the sixth straight season the program had been good enough for the NCAA Tournament. All indications were that 2010 could be even better.

But during the off-season the head Frog didn't like what he saw at all. Apparently, "a gaudy preseason ranking after reaching the Super Regionals the season before made some players question the need for fundamental drills." Some players were late to workouts, and overall the team's training effort was little more than halfhearted.

So Schlossnagle acted, apparently reasoning that if the team wasn't giving its best, then it didn't deserve the best facilities. The head coach kicked the players out of their own place for a week. No locker room and no weight room. They couldn't even get onto the turf of Lupton Stadium.

Senior team captain Bryan Holaday, who would win the Johnny Bench award as college baseball's best catcher, wasn't one bit happy about the situation. He called a players-only meeting and told them they would be working out on "the hill," the grassy field northwest of the stadium. "I told coach, 'I don't care what you say, we're practicing,'" Holaday said.

If the whole business was a clever Schlossnagle ploy, it worked. The Frogs set a school record with 54 wins and advanced to the College World Series for the first time ever.

That civic club with membership by invitation only. The bleachers where you sit while others frolic in the sky boxes. That neighborhood you can't afford a house in. You know all about being shut out of some club, some group, some place. "Exclusive" is the word that keeps you out.

The Hebrew people, too, knew about being told to keep out; only the high priest enter the Most Holy Place – which housed the ark -- and survive. Then along came Jesus to kick that barrier down and give us direct access to God.

In the process, though, Jesus created another exclusive club; its members are his followers, Christians, those who believe he is the Son of God and the savior of the world. This club, though, extends a membership invitation to everyone in the whole wide world; no one is excluded. Whether you're in or out depends on your response to Jesus, not on arbitrary gatekeepers.

We needed a jolt to get back to what this program is based on. If that hadn't happened, I don't know what we would have done.
        -- Bryan Holaday on being kicked out of the team facilities

**Christianity is an exclusive club, but an invitation
is extended to everyone and no one is denied entry.**

ANIMAL MAGNETISM

Read Psalm 139:1-18.

"For you created my inmost being; you knit me together in my mother's womb. I praise you because I am fearfully and wonderfully made" (vv. 13-14).

One thing for sure: TCU has the only mascot that can spit blood out of its eyes.

The horned frog has been TCU's mascot longer than the school has been TCU. School lore has it that the horned frog and AddRan Christian University, which became Texas Christian University in 1902, first teamed up in 1896.

As the legend goes, the unimproved field on which the school's first football team practiced was overrun with the varmints. The playful students imitated the fierce-looking critters by scampering around and soon began referring to themselves as horned frogs. The name stuck. A less romantic story has it that Addison Clark, Jr., son of one of the school's founders and the man most responsible for bringing football to TCU, (See Devotion No. 1.) was fascinated with horned frogs and probably influenced the decision to make the sturdy little creatures the mascot.

The horned frog is neither a frog nor a toad but is actually a small lizard, no more than three to five inches long, that feeds off 80 to 100 red harvester ants a day. They are cold-blooded reptiles and have a gland that resembles a third eye on the top of their head. Scientists believe this unusual feature helps them regulate

HORNED FROGS

their body temperature. And as bizarre as it sounds, horned frogs really *can* squirt a fine four-foot long steam of blood from their eyes when they are angry or frightened.

The campus entered a new bronze age on March 13, 2013, with the dedication of a new 8-foot-tall statue of a horned frog outside the east entrance of Amon G. Carter Stadium. One blogger called the sculpture "the apex of intimidation." This ferocious frog joined the statue installed in 1984 that has ever since provided good luck to students who rub its nose before tests.

Animals such as the horned frog elicit our awe and our respect. Nothing enlivens a trip more than glimpsing animals in the wild. Admit it: You go along with the kids' trip to the zoo because you think it's a cool place too. All that variety of life is mind-boggling. Who could conceive of a horned frog, a moose, or a prairie dog? Who could possibly have that rich an imagination?

But the next time you're in a crowd, look around at the parade of faces. Who could come up with the idea for all those different people? For that matter, who could ever conceive of you? You are unique, a masterpiece who will never be duplicated.

The master creator, God Almighty, is behind it all. He thought of you and brought you into being. If you had come into this world with a manufacturer's label, it might say, "Lovingly, fearfully, and wonderfully hand-made in Heaven by #1 -- God."

Be kind dear friend do not abuse a little Horned Frog. Remember you've a friend in me, the little Horned Frog.
-- from the preface to the 1906 TCU yearbook

Paintings and magnificent animals are works of art, but the real masterpiece is you.

DAY 48

THE RIGHT MAN

Read Exodus 3:1-12.

"So now, go. I am sending you to Pharaoh to bring my people the Israelites out of Egypt" (v. 10).

Not everyone thought Gary Patterson was the right man for the job.

Patterson arrived at TCU in 1998 as Dennis Franchione's defensive coordinator. In their third season together, the Frogs won ten games and a second straight WAC title, and Patterson's defense was statistically the best in the country.

After that, Franchione left for Alabama. Patterson stayed in Fort Worth, hoping for a shot at being named the head Frog. But Eric Hyman, TCU's athletics director, had his sights set on the head coach at Alabama-Birmingham.

Dick Lowe and Herb Zimmerman, who had played for Dutch Meyer in the 1950s, were on the athletic committee, and they liked what they had seen of Patterson. Provost Bill Koehler was also in Patterson's corner. While lifting weights in the Walsh Complex, he had repeatedly heard the players praise their defensive boss.

Hyman recommended his man from Alabama-Birmingham to the trustees. Koehler, Lowe, and Zimmerman persisted, though, and Hyman ultimately relented and got behind Patterson. The trustees unanimously approved the hire.

Doubts persisted during Patterson's inaugural season of 2001. After a loss at home to a lower-division school, grumbling TCU

HORNED FROGS

supporters gathered outside the Frog locker room and collectively asked, "Are you sure we have the right guy?"

They did. On. Sept. 9, 2012, Patterson's 20th-ranked Frogs beat Grambling State 56-0 for his 110th win, the most in school history for any head football coach. Moreover, heading into the 2013 season as the top Frog, he had led TCU to a golden age the likes of which had not been seen for decades.

Gary Patterson was definitely the right man for the job.

What do you want to be when you grow up? Somehow you are supposed to know the answer to that question when you're a teenager, the time in life when common sense and logic are at their lowest ebb. Long after those halcyon teen years are left behind, you may make frequent career changes. You chase the job that gives you not just financial rewards but also some personal satisfaction and sense of accomplishment.

God, too, wants you in the right job, one that he has designed specifically for you. Though Moses protested that he wasn't the right man, he was indeed God's anointed one, the right man to do exactly what God needed done.

There's a little Moses in all of us. Like him, we shrink before the tasks God calls us to. Like him also, we have God-given abilities, talents, and passions. The right man or women for any job is the one who works and achieves, not for self but for the glory of God.

He's been remarkable for TCU and his record speaks for itself.
-- Former TCU athletics director Eric Hyman on Gary Patterson

**Working for God's glory and not your own
makes you the right person for the job,
no matter what it may be.**

WEATHERPROOFED

Read Nahum 1:3-9.

"His way is in the whirlwind and the storm, and clouds are the dust of his feet" (v. 3b).

The weather and the refs may have conspired to keep the Frogs from winning a game, but they couldn't keep TCU from winning a championship.

Oct. 20, 1956 dawned bright and sunny. The forecast for TCU's game with Texas A&M called for a slight chance of rain with temperatures in the 80s. Boy, was that wrong.

"Strangest game I ever played in," said Frog quarterback Chuck Curtis. "The day started off real nice. . . . Then it started raining. Then it started hailing. Then it got dark, the wind came up, and we had a tornado." By halftime, half of the capacity crowd "had fled in terror." As Curtis remembered it, for some of the game, he'd call the signals at the line, "but no one could hear them because of the hail bouncing off their helmets."

During the worst of the weather, TCU drove to a third down on the A&M 3. All-American halfback Jim Swink apparently scored, but one official said no and placed the ball inches from the goal line. All-conference fullback Buddy Dike had no doubts that Swink scored. "I know, because I led the play and I was lying in the end zone and Swink was lying there with me, clutching my shirttail," he said.

Guard Vernon Uecker also insisted that Swink was in. "He was past me, and I was lying on the goal line," he said. One official close to the play indicated Swink was across the goal, but another ref disagreed. "The official who made the call came running from across the field, with rain splattering all over his glasses," Uecker remembered.

When A&M held on fourth down, the Aggies went on to win 7-6 in what has entered TCU lore as "The Hurricane Game." Playing in better weather, the Frogs rallied to finish 7-3, win the league title outright, and beat Syracuse in the Cotton Bowl.

A thunderstorm washes away your golf game or the picnic with the kids. Lightning knocks out the electricity just as you settle in at the computer. A tornado interrupts your Sunday dinner and sends everyone scurrying to the hallway. A hurricane blows away your beach trip.

For all our technology and our knowledge, we are still at the mercy of the weather, able only to get a little more advance warning than in the past. The weather answers only to God. Rain and hail will fall where they want to, totally inconsiderate of something as important as a TCU football game.

We stand mute before the awesome power of the weather, but we should be even more awestruck at the power of the one who controls it, a power beyond our imagining. Neither, however, can we imagine the depths of God's love for us, a love that drove him to die on a cross for us.

You had to turn your head to breathe.
-- TCU halfback Jim Swink on how hard it was raining

The power of the one who controls the weather is unimaginable, but so is his love for us.

HOMEBODIES

Read 2 Corinthians 5:1-10.

"We . . . would prefer to be away from the body and at home with the Lord" (v. 8).

Feeling out of place and challenged in her faith, Kortnie Maxoutopoulis transferred and found a home at TCU.

When she was being recruited as a high school golfer, Maxoutopoulis visited TCU but at the time had decided she was not interested in schools outside her native California. A school trip to Washington, D.C., changed her mind, however. She realized that "college was a good time to try something new, so I started looking out of state." She wound up at Rutgers, enticed by the 40-minute drive from the campus to New York City and by the golf program itself.

Maxoutopoulis never felt at home in New Jersey. Athletically, the tournaments didn't live up to her expectations. "I felt if I would have stayed, I would have just been settling," she said. But there was more. Personally, she felt that her deep faith left her in a place she didn't belong.

So she began looking around. She seriously considered Maryland and Oregon, but decided on TCU because of its size and the golf program's structure. She arrived in January 2013 and was eligible to play in the spring.

In Fort Worth, Maxoutopoulis found the golf home she had been looking for. "She came to us," said head coach Angie Ravaioli-Larkin. "She really fit with what we were looking for as far as talent and discipline on and off the golf course."

Maxoutopoulis also found the spiritual home she had been seeking. At TCU, she felt free to declare how important her faith was in her life, to enjoy open discussions about faith with her teammates, and to listen to Christian music before she headed off to class.

"I'm not playing for myself," Maxoutopoulis said. "I'm playing for [God], and knowing that calms me down on the course." She thus felt right at home and relaxed enough to crack the golf team's regular lineup as a sophomore in 2013.

Home is not necessarily a matter of geography. It may be that place you share with your spouse and your children, whether it's Texas or New Jersey. You may feel at home when you return to Fort Worth, wondering why you were so eager to leave in the first place. Maybe the home you grew up in still feels like an old shoe, a little worn but comfortable and inviting.

God planted that sense of home in us because he is a God of place, and our place is with him. Thus, we may live a few blocks away from our parents and grandparents or we may relocate every few years, but we will still sometimes feel as though we don't really belong no matter where we are. We don't; our true home is with God in the place Jesus has gone ahead to prepare for us. We are homebodies and we are perpetually homesick.

The program here is more intense and structured, which I thrive off of.
– Kortnie Maxoutopoulis on finding a home at TCU

We are continually homesick for our real home, which is with God in Heaven.

WHAT A SURPRISE!

Read 1 Thessalonians 5:1-11.

"But you, brothers, are not in darkness so that this day should surprise you like a thief" (v. 4).

Nick Browne was surprised to find his name at the top of the kickers' depth chart, but he probably wasn't nearly as surprised as his coaches were.

When the TCU football coaches went looking for a placekicker following the 2000 season, they didn't have to go far. They just took a short walk over to the university's soccer field. There they found Nick Browne and his powerful left foot. Special teams coach Dan Sharp was much like the other coaches, though; he wasn't too keen on converting a soccer player into the team's primary place-kicker. Browne's attitude and his foot changed Sharp's mind.

Browne was all for it. "I have always loved football," he said, but he wasn't recruited "because I was on a high school team that didn't win much and didn't go to football camps."

So Browne walked on in the spring of 2000 and found himself at the bottom of the six-man depth chart. Halfway through spring practice of 2001, though, he walked into the locker room one day and -- to his surprise -- found his name at the top of the list.

TCU head coach Gary Patterson was just as surprised. Shortly before the 2001 season began, he strolled into Sharp's office and asked him who would be handling kicking duties. Sharp tossed out Browne's name. "Who?" Patterson asked.

HORNED FROGS

It didn't take the head Frog long to figure out who Browne was. Along with Ross Evans (2008-11), he is one of the greatest kickers in school history. He was a First-Team All-America as a senior in 2003 and Conference USA's Special Teams Player of the Year. Among the school records he still holds are points and field goals in a season (122 and 28 in 2003) and career field goals (65).

Nick Browne was one of those really good surprises.

Surprise birthday parties are a delight. And what's the fun of opening Christmas presents when we already know what's in them? Some surprises in life provide us with experiences that are both joyful and delightful.

Generally, though, we expend energy and resources to avoid most surprises and the impact they may have upon our lives. We may be surprised by the exact timing of a baby's arrival, but we nevertheless have the bags packed beforehand and the nursery all set for its occupant. Paul used this very image (v. 3) to describe the Day of the Lord, when Jesus will return to claim his own and establish his kingdom. We may be caught by surprise, but we must still be ready.

The consequences of being caught unprepared by a baby's insistence on being born are serious indeed. They pale, however, beside the eternal effects of not being ready when Jesus returns. We prepare ourselves just as Paul told us to (v. 8): We live in faith, hope, and love, ever on the alert for that great, promised day.

Wow, I didn't expect that!
-- Nick Browne on finding his name at the top of the depth chart in 2001

The timing of Jesus' return will be a surprise; the consequences should not be.

UNDERDOG

Read 1 Samuel 17:17-50.

"David said to the Philistine, . . . 'This day the Lord will hand you over to me, and I'll strike you down'" (vv. 45-46).

They were young, those Frogs, but that didn't keep them from acting like David and felling a mighty giant.

Writer Gil LeBreton dubbed it "the most memorable Thanksgiving night in the school's 117 years of football." He was speaking of 2012 and the night TCU "outfought, outplayed, outcoached and outshined" the heavily favored Texas Longhorns in Austin.

"We've grown up," head coach Gary Patterson said after the 20-13 win that pushed TCU to 7-4 for the season and dropped Texas to 8-3. "We're a lot more mature." But they were still young, so young that sixteen freshmen played in the game. The quarterback who led his team to the win -- Trevone Boykin -- was a redshirt freshman.

Patterson nevertheless refused to proclaim the win over the Big 12's most storied program the greatest win in TCU's history. After he emerged from the uproarious TCU locker room, the head Frog wouldn't even agree that his team was the underdog. He said that if he declared the win to be a milestone, "then I'd be admitting that I didn't think we could do it." He chastised the media, the alums, and the fans for giving the other guys too much credit. "We've played in a lot of ballgames like this." A Rose Bowl trophy in his office verifies the truth of his statement.

Still, a young TCU squad went into Austin on national TV and was the better team. Boykin "stole the night's show." He had 77 yards rushing and 82 passing, completing 7 of 9 chunks. The rest of the night belonged to the defense, led by All-Big 12 linebacker Kenny Cain, who had fourteen tackles.

TCU dominated the giant all night long. With only five minutes to play, the Frogs led by two touchdowns and had held Texas to slightly more than 200 yards of total offense.

Consider the giant slain.

You probably don't gird your loins, pick up a slingshot and some smooth, round river rocks, and go out to battle ill-tempered giants regularly. You do, however, fight each day to make some economic and social progress and to keep the ones you love safe, sheltered, and protected. Armed only with your pluck, your knowledge, your wits, and your hustle, in many ways you are an underdog; the best you can hope for is that the world is indifferent. You need all the weapons you can get.

How about using the ultimate weapon David had: the absolute, unshakable conviction that when he tackled opposition of any size, he would prevail. He knew this because he did everything for God's glory and therefore God was in his corner.

If you imitate David's lifestyle by glorifying God in everything you do, then God is there for you when you need him. Who's the underdog then?

Remember that Goliath was a 40-point favorite over Little David.
-- Legendary Auburn football coach Shug Jordan

Living to glorify God is the lifestyle of a winner.

DAY 53

HERO WORSHIP

Read 1 Samuel 16:1-13.

"Do not consider his appearance or his height, for . . . the Lord does not look at the things man looks at. . . . The Lord looks at the heart" (v. 7).

Former TCU track star Kim Collins was such a hero in his home country that he even had his own postage stamp.

Collins was a sprinter for the Frog track teams of 2000-2001; he won three NCAA titles (individual and relay) and received six All-America certificates. He joined Raymond Stewart (1985-89) as the only TCU athletes in school history to win two individual NCAA titles.

Though Collins competed in the Summer Olympics four times, the biggest triumph of his career came in the 2003 World Championships when he won the 100-meter sprint by 0.01 seconds. With that win, Collins became the first world champion from his home country, St. Kitts and Nevis. The island federation in the Caribbean is the tiniest sovereign state in the Americas with a population of slightly more than 50,000. In honor of their hero, the nation threw Collins a party when he returned home.

Aug. 25, the date of his championship run, was designated as Kim Collins Day throughout the country. He had a private meeting with the prime minister, received a new house and an SUV (which he could drive down the Kim Collins Highway), had an athletic facility named after him, and had his likeness plastered on a postage stamp. "The entire nation has come together to celebrate," Collins said.

Those 2003 World Championships wound up as something of a TCU reunion. In addition to Collins, among those present were Darvis Patton, a 10-time All-American; former TCU head coach Bubba Thornton who coached the U.S. team; and then-current and former Frogs Michael Frater, Brandon Simpson, Jon Drummond, Ricardo Williams, Bev McDonald, and Khadevis Robinson.

A hero is commonly thought of as someone who performs extraordinary acts -- as Kim Collins did in becoming the fastest man alive -- or brave and dangerous feats that save or protect someone's life. You figure that excludes you.

But ask your son about that when you show him how to bait a hook or throw a football, or your daughter when you show up for her honors night at school. Look into the eyes of those Little Leaguers you help coach.

Ask God about heroism when you're steady in your faith. For God, a hero is a person with the heart of a servant. And if a hero is a servant who acts to save other's lives, then the greatest hero of all is Jesus Christ.

God seeks heroes today, those who will proclaim the name of their hero – Jesus – proudly and boldly, no matter how others may scoff or ridicule. God knows heroes when he sees them -- by what's in their hearts.

This is the biggest thing that ever happened to the island.
                    -- Kim Collins on his 2003 world championship

**God's heroes are those who remain steady
in their faith while serving others.**

TEACHER'S PET

Read John 3:1-16.

"[Nicodemus] came to Jesus at night and said, 'Rabbi, we know you are a teacher who has come from God'" (v. 2).

TCU head coach Gary Patterson didn't stop teaching, not even after a 35-point blowout.

At a glance, TCU's 56-21 rout of Texas State on Sept. 19, 2009, seems pretty routine. The 15th-ranked Frogs got the win in their home opener against the Bobcats from the Football Championship Subdivision. All-Mountain West running back Joseph Turner rushed for 129 yards and three touchdowns on only thirteen carries. Senior Jerry Hughes, a two-time All-America and two-time conference defensive player of the year, had three sacks. He would go on to win the Ted Hendricks Award as college football's best defensive end.

Overall, Patterson admitted he was happy with the win, but he also knew that "he was going to be upset with his team by Sunday morning after reviewing the film." Why? "We didn't play the way we needed to," he said.

He had a point. The undermanned Bobcats stayed close to the Frogs on into the third quarter primarily because of TCU mistakes. When Antoine Hicks scored on a 4-yard run early in the second half, TCU led quite comfortably 35-14. But Texas State wasn't ready to concede. The Bobcats scored and then got the ball back on a fumble. Jason Teague's interception in the end zone kept Texas State from closing to within a touchdown. Only in the fourth quarter did TCU put the game away with three touchdown runs from Turner, Matthew Tucker, and Jercell Fort.

Thus, Patterson knew his players had much to learn from the game. "We have to have attention to detail; we have to communicate. We have the potential to be what we want to be," he said. In other words, he had some teaching to do. Apparently he did it quite well. TCU would go 12-0, win the conference, land its first BCS bowl, and finish as the 6th-ranked team in the country.

You can read this book, break 90 on the golf course, and do your job well because somebody taught you. And as you learn, you become the teacher yourself. You teach your children how to play Monopoly and how to drive a car. You show rookies the ropes at the office and teach baseball's basics to Little Leaguers.

This pattern of learning and then teaching includes your spiritual life also. Somebody taught you about Jesus, and this, too, you must pass on. Jesus came to teach a truth the religious teachers and the powerful of his day did not want to hear. Little has changed in that regard; the world today often reacts with scorn and disdain to Jesus' message.

Nothing, not even death itself, could stop Jesus from teaching his lesson of life and salvation. So should nothing stop you from teaching life's most important lesson: Jesus saves.

It will be good for us, will get us to focus more.
-- Jerry Hughes on Gary Patterson's lessons from the Texas State game

In life, you learn and then you teach,
which includes learning and teaching about Jesus,
the most important lesson of all.

A HEX ON YOU

Read Jonah 1.

"Tell us, who is responsible for making all this trouble for us? What did you do?" (v. 8a)

Forty-thousand red candles. Such were the tools Texas Longhorn fans used to hex the Horned Frogs. It didn't work.

Prior to the game of Nov. 12, 1955, anxious Texas fans were willing to try anything that might help defeat favored TCU. So they tried hexing the Frogs by burning some 40,000 red candles. Their team would have been better off tackling TCU All-American Jim Swink.

But they didn't. Against Texas, the junior halfback, runner-up for the Heisman Trophy that season, had a career day, rushing for 235 yards and scoring four touchdowns "in one of the most brilliant one-man shows in conference history."

He had plenty of help, though, from junior quarterback Charles "Chuck" Curtis, who threw three touchdown passes on his way to an All-Southwest Conference season. The two of them led the way in "putting on the largest scoring circus any Southwest Conference team ever marshalled against the Longhorns."

The Frogs won 47-20. So much for a hex.

The game was actually close until the fourth quarter. TCU led only 20-14 before suddenly exploding for 27 points in the final period. On the first play of the quarter, Curtis dropped a perfect spiral into the waiting arms of senior receiver Bryan Engram for a 30-yard touchdown. The rout was on.

Two minutes later, Curtis found junior end O'Day Williams with another 30-yard scoring strike. After that, Swink finished off the Horns with a pair of scoring runs.

The Frogs went 9-1 that season, won the conference title, and wound up fifth in the nation. Center/linebacker Hugh Pitts joined Swink as All-America.

As that 1955 game against Texas clearly demonstrates, hexes, jinxes, and the like really belong to the domain of superstitious balderdash. Some people do feel, however, that they exist under a dark and rainy cloud. Nothing goes right; all their dreams collapse around them; they seem to constantly bring about misery on themselves and also on the ones around them.

Why? Is it really a hex, a jinx?

Nonsense. The Bible provides us an excellent example in Jonah. Those around him – namely the sailors on the boat with him -- believed him to be a hex who doomed them all. Jonah's life was a big mess, but it had nothing to do with a jinx. His life was in shambles because he was disobeying God.

Take a careful look at people you know whose lives are like Jonah's, including some who profess to believe in God. The key to life lies not just in believing; the responsibility of the believer is to obey God. Problems lie not in hexes but in disobedience.

All week, thousands of Longhorn [fans] burned red candles to put the Frogs under the spell that enabled Texas to overcome formidable foes.
-- Writer Flem Hall

Hexes don't cause us trouble,
but disobedience to God sure does.

SIZE MATTERS

Read Luke 19:1-10.

"[Zacchaeus] wanted to see who Jesus was, but being a short man he could not, because of the crowd. So he ran ahead and climbed a sycamore-fig tree to see him" (vv. 3-4).

Davey O'Brien was no giant, but in 1938 he was the biggest man in college football.

A senior quarterback in 1938, O'Brien had one of the greatest seasons in the history of college football. He powered the Frogs to an 11-0 season and both the conference and the national titles, the first time in history that a team from the Southwest Conference had won the national championship. He led the nation in passing and total offense. He then became the first player in SWC history to win the Heisman Trophy and the only player in SWC history to win the Heisman, the Maxwell Trophy as the College Player of the Year, and the Walter Camp Award as the Player of the Year in the same season.

In 1938, Davey O'Brien was truly *the* Big Man on Campus.

So how in the world could his nickname be "Little Davey"? Quarterback Davey O'Brien, the ultimate giant killer, stood only 5-foot-7 and weighed only 150 pounds.

Don Looney, one of O'Brien's favorite receivers said, "There were a lot of times that I would go out for a pass and look back for Davey -- and I couldn't see him. Then all of a sudden the ball would come flying out of nowhere -- right into my arms."

O'Brien could run with the ball, but he also stood big in the pocket like no quarterback before him. Guard Mason Mayne, inducted into the TCU Letterman's Hall of Fame in 1975, said O'Brien "was one of the first players I ever saw who [could] stay in the pocket and concentrate on throwing the ball despite the rush. He used to say he didn't want to get away from his friends."

Davey O'Brien always stood tall.

Bigger is better! Such is one of the most powerful mantras of our time. We expand our football stadiums. We augment our body parts. Hey, make that a triple cheeseburger and a large order of fries! My company is bigger than your company. Even our church buildings must be bigger to be better. About the only exception to our all-consuming drive for bigness is our waistlines.

But size obviously didn't matter to Jesus. After all, salvation came to the house of an evil tax collector who was so short he had to climb a tree to catch a glimpse of Jesus. Zacchaeus indeed had a big bank account; he was a big man in town even if his own people scorned him. But none of that – including Zacchaeus' height – mattered; Zacchaeus received salvation because of his repentance, which revealed itself in a changed life.

The same is true for us today. What matters is the size of the heart devoted to our Lord.

I never thought of Davey [O'Brien] as being small. He had wide shoulders and a lot of muscle packed into that body. And he was tough.
-- Sammy Baugh

Size matters to Jesus, but only the size
of the heart of the one who would follow Him.

THE PIONEER SPIRIT

Read Luke 5:1-11.

"So they pulled their boats up on shore, left everything and followed him" (v. 11).

Fourteen young women and an English professor -- and they didn't even have a basketball. But they were pioneers.

In the fall of 1974, associate professor of English Bob Frye was asked to coach TCU's first-ever women's basketball team. He apparently received the honor because he had been on basketball scholarship at Wayland Baptist College, which had a dominating women's basketball team in the 1940s-50s.

He was paid $1,000 and had a budget of $835. What he didn't have was any scholarships, uniforms, or basketballs. Men's basketball coach Johnny Swain kicked in four balls, and the TCU House of Representatives supported the pioneers by approving $50 for two more.

The first uniforms were mix and match. Some were blue, not purple. Frye did locate four purple tops, and his wife found some matching material at a local fabric shop and sewed some shorts. "When we suited up we seemed a hymn to diversity," Frye said.

Twenty-two women showed up for tryouts, including the vice chancellor's daughter, who promptly broke her arm. Fourteen players made the first-ever team. Frye worked out a 15-game schedule and arranged for the use of two school station wagons for transportation. He drove one, his wife the other.

HORNED FROGS

When that first team entered a state tournament at Stephenville, they didn't have the funds to spend the night. So they had to drive home after playing and then leave the next morning at 5:30 to play an 8 a.m. game.

Let the record show that on Dec. 6, 1974, women's basketball at TCU officially began with a 71-36 win over Richland College.

Going to a place in your life you've never been before requires a willingness to take risks and face uncertainty head-on. Perhaps you never helped start a new sports program at a major college, but you've had your moments when your latent pioneer spirit manifested itself. That time you changed careers, ran a marathon, volunteered at a homeless shelter, learned Spanish, or went back to school.

While attempting new things invariably begets apprehension, the truth is that when life becomes too comfortable and too familiar, it gets boring. The same is true of God, who is downright dangerous because he calls us to be anything but comfortable as we serve him. He summons us to continuously blaze new trails in our faith life, to follow him no matter what.

Stepping out on faith is risky all right, but the reward is a life of accomplishment, adventure, and joy that cannot be equaled anywhere else.

I frequently looked up from our bench in Daniel-Meyer to see five or six people, total, in the stands.
-- Bob Frye on the first season of women's basketball at TCU

Unsafe and downright dangerous, God calls us out of the place where we are comfortable to a life of adventure and trailblazing in his name.

IN THE KNOW

Read John 4:19-26, 39-42.

*"They said to the woman, . . . 'Now we have heard for
ourselves, and we know that this man really is the Savior
of the world'" (v. 42).*

Stanley Washington just knew. What happened after that is
TCU legend.

On Oct. 3, 1981, with 5:20 left on the clock, the Frogs trailed
Arkansas 24-13. They had the ball, but it sat 99 yards away from
the Hog goal line. Disappointed fans had already started to leave
the stadium. TCU needed somebody to make some plays.

Washington was usually that somebody. The player KILLER-
FROGS.com named in 2012 as the second-greatest receiver in
TCU history (behind Mike Renfro) was an All-American in 1981.
He entered the Arkansas game as the nation's leading receiver.
This day, though, he did not have a single reception.

Before Washington ran onto the field with time running out
and his team in trouble, reserve placekicker John Denton told him,
"We need those magic hands of yours. If you got anything left in
those hands of yours, let us have it." "I started to get that feeling,"
Washington said. He knew he was going to score.

From the Razorback 42, quarterback Steve Stamp found Washington running open down the left sideline for 20 yards. On the
next play, Washington broke loose again, this time in the corner
of the end zone, and Stamp got him the ball. Tight end Bob Fields

hauled in the two-point conversion, and TCU trailed only 24-21.

When freshman safety Byron Linwood recovered an Arkansas fumble, TCU had a chance for a win with under three minutes left. On third-and-10 at the Hog 15, Washington lined up at tight end and broke open. "He was wide open," Stamp said. "It was just a matter of hitting him." Stamp did.

After Washington "got the feeling" and just knew he was going to score, he caught three passes, two for touchdowns, and TCU had a miraculous 28-24 win.

Stanley Washington just knew that day in the same way you know certain things in your life. That your spouse loves you, for instance. That you are good at your job. That a bad day fishing is still better than a good day at work. You know these things even though no mathematician or philosopher can prove any of this on paper.

It's the same way with faith in Jesus: You just know that he is God's son and the savior of the world. You know it in the same way that you know TCU is really the only team worth pulling for: with every fiber of your being, with all your heart, your mind, and your soul. You know it despite the mindless babble and blasphemy of the unbelievers.

You just know, and because you know him, Jesus knows you. And that is all you really need to know.

I got the feeling that if I touched the ball, I was going to get it into the end zone.
> -- Stanley Washington, who just knew against Arkansas

A life of faith is lived in certainty and conviction:
You just know that you know.

THE BIG MO

Read 2 Chronicles 7:11-22.

*"If my people, . . . will humble themselves and pray and
seek my face and turn from their wicked ways, then will I
hear from heaven and will forgive their sin" (v. 14).*

One play gave the Frogs the momentum they needed to come
from behind and beat Texas.

On Nov. 18, 1967, the Horned Frogs trailed Texas in Austin 17-6
as the fourth quarter began, a deficit that looked as though it was
too much to overcome. Until Bubba Thornton broke loose and set
in motion the momentum that led to an 18-point fourth quarter.

Thornton was a junior college transfer who hadn't played a
down until the Baylor game three weeks before the trip to Austin.
With 12:15 to play, he gathered in a Longhorn punt at the TCU
22. That was only after fellow safety Mike Hall had yelled at him
first to take it and then to "Follow me, follow me." Hall knocked
the first defender away from Thornton, who then followed his
blockers for a 78-yard touchdown. "Don't give me credit," Thornton said after the game. "Give it to the blockers."

His return fired up a previously moribund TCU team. "You
could feel something on the sideline," declared senior linebacker
E.A. Gresham. "It was like an electric current sweeping through
everyone."

Quarterback P.D. Shabay and Bill Ferguson, who would be inducted into the TCU Lettermen's Hall of Fame, connected for the

2-point conversion. Suddenly, it was 17-14, and the Frog pond was hopping. Sophomore Wayne Merritt booted a 29-yard field goal with 6:10 left to tie the game. Then with only 61 seconds on the clock, fullback Kenny Post plowed through the Texas defense for a 1-yard touchdown.

The momentum Thornton's return generated carried TCU all the way to a 24-17 win.

Unlike a football game, momentum in life usually doesn't happen suddenly. Any small business owner can talk of the early struggles before his enterprise became successful. We build our careers over the decades, moving up from entry-level positions. It's an old truism that maintaining success is harder than getting it; in other words, keeping our momentum requires work.

This is true in our faith lives also. We are all called by God to spiritual greatness -- to a life of achieving extraordinary things for him that, in turn, spills over into achievements in other areas of our daily lives. Too many of us don't attain it, however. We may start out on fire for the Lord, but we sputter and fall short, overwhelmed by the challenges before us. We lose our momentum.

Even with our dreams surrendered, our lives stagnant, and our hopes dashed, we have a ready answer: Turn back to God. We can intentionally choose God's direction for our lives and turn back to the godly lifestyle that established our momentum in the first place.

That gave us the momentum.
                    -- E.A. Gresham on Bubba Thornton's punt return

**With our lives going nowhere, we can turn
back to God for direction and momentum.**

THE COMEBACK

Read Luke 23:26-43.

"Jesus answered him, 'I tell you the truth, today you will be with me in paradise'" (v. 43).

Texas Christian's long comeback to college football greatness was completed on some of the game's most hallowed turf.

When the Southwest Conference fell apart in 1994, TCU was "abandoned on the doorstep," an orphan nobody really wanted. The school's fall from college football's penthouse had been years in the making before that. The plunge included "the tragedy of coach Jim Pittman's death on the sideline in 1971 (See Devotion No. 33.), . . . the collapse of the program later in the '70s and the bitter NCAA sanctions handed to it in 1986."

It took a while, but the Frogs came back, completing the journey on Saturday, January 1, 2011, when they beat Wisconsin 21-19 in the Rose Bowl. Tight ends coach Dan Sharp described what that game meant to TCU: "It took so long, and we've come so far. And we're here. It's unbelievable."

The win was no fluke. The Frogs didn't have a single turnover. They held the Badgers -- who had scored 83 points on Indiana and 70 on Northwestern -- to 19 points. Like the conference and BSC bowl champions they were, the Horned Frogs made the big plays when they had to, the biggest of them all Tank Carder's swatting away of Wisconsin's pass on the try for the game-tying 2-point conversion with two minutes left.

HORNED FROGS

When those interminable 120 seconds finally ticked away, the confetti rained, and the hugs, the shouts, and the tears began. Caps and T-shirts proclaimed "TCU 2011 Rose Bowl Champions."

In the locker room, head coach Gary Patterson held up his cellphone and ordered, "Look at this." The phone read "175 text messages. Network authenticity failed." The Frogs had not only shaken the status quo of college football to its foundation but had shut down an entire phone network.

The Horned Frogs were back -- bigger and better than ever.

Life will have its setbacks whether they result from personal failures or from forces and people beyond your control. Being a Christian and a faithful follower of Jesus Christ doesn't insulate you from getting into deep trouble. Maybe financial problems suffocated you. A serious illness sidelined you. Or your family was hit with a great tragedy. Life is a series of victories and defeats. Winning isn't about avoiding defeat; it's about getting back up to compete again. It's about making a comeback of your own.

When you avail yourself of God's grace and God's power, your comeback is always greater than your setback. You are never too far behind, and it's never too late in life's game for Jesus to lead you to victory, to turn trouble into triumph. As it was with the Horned Frogs and the thief on the cross who repented, it's not how you start that counts; it's how you finish.

One of college football's greatest comeback stories had written a unique and glorious chapter.
-- Writer Gil LeBreton on the 2011 Rose Bowl

In life, victory is truly a matter of how you finish and whether you finish with Jesus at your side.

REST EASY

Read Hebrews 4:1-11.

"There remains, then, a Sabbath rest for the people of God; for anyone who enters God's rest also rests from his own work, just as God did from his. Let us, therefore, make every effort to enter that rest" (vv. 9-11).

A horrendously broken leg gave TCU golfer Eli Cole the time off he needed to improve his game.

Despite sending e-mails to a number of college coaches, Cole was virtually unrecruited out of high school. He knew nothing of TCU, and Frog coaches had never heard of him. Head coach Bill Montigel made a trip to California to recruit one of Cole's best friends, who opted for another program. To avoid wasting the trip, Montigel asked the recruit's swing coach if he knew anyone else he could recommend. He named Cole.

Cole worked his way into the lineup during his sophomore season of 2009-10 and was a regular as a junior. Back home during the summer, however, he broke his leg in two places while playing soccer at a friend's birthday party. "The minute it happened, I just started thinking how long it was going to take me to get back to playing," he said.

It took a while. The break ultimately required three surgeries, and it was eleven months before Cole could play 18 holes while walking and carrying his own bag. He didn't waste the time.

With his typical work ethic, he studied, watched sophomore

All-American Julien Brun play, and asked questions. The injury gave him the time to focus on details that most players overlook and to learn more about the game.

After a redshirt season, he returned in 2012-13 and had the best year of his TCU career. He was named to the All-Central Region Team and helped the Frogs finish 19th in the NCAA Tournament.

In retrospect, Montigel called Cole's injury a blessing. The time off "made his game a lot better," the coach said.

As part of the natural rhythm of life, rest is important to maintain physical health. Rest has different images, though: a good eight hours in the sack; a leisurely Saturday morning that begins in the backyard with the paper and a pot of coffee; a vacation in the mountains. Or just a break from the stress and pace of daily living, even if that rat race includes collegiate golf.

Rest is also part of the rhythm and the health of our spiritual lives. Often we envision the truly faithful person as always busy, always doing something for God whether it's teaching Sunday school or showing up at church every time the doors open.

But God himself rested from work, and in blessing us with the Sabbath, he calls us into a time of rest. To rest by simply spending time in the presence of God is to receive spiritual revitalization and rejuvenation. Sleep refreshes your body and your mind; God's rest refreshes your soul.

I took that period to try and do some research to figure out what I needed to do better.
-- Eli Cole on the time off his injury gave him

God promises you a spiritual rest
that renews and refreshes your soul.

GREAT EXPECTATIONS

Read John 1:43-51.

"'Nazareth! Can anything good come from there?'
Nathanael asked" (v. 46).

Jeff Ballard had some pretty set expectations for the 2005 football season. They didn't quite work out.

When the season began, Ballard, a junior quarterback, was right where he expected to be: on the sideline talking with the starter, senior Tye Gunn. He might see a little action sometime during the season, perhaps in a blowout. "I felt like Tye would start all 11 games and play well the entire year," Ballard said.

Ballard's expectations were realistic. He had attempted only one pass as a Frog and was a virtual unknown. In 2004, when both Gunn and Brandon Hassell were injured, Kyle Kummer, and not Ballard, stepped into the starting role.

Midway through the third quarter against BYU, Ballard's expectations changed dramatically. The 2-1 Frogs trailed by 18 points when Gunn went down with a separated shoulder. Suddenly, the offense belonged to Ballard.

He was an instant hero. This virtual unknown guided TCU to five straight touchdowns in regulation and overtime, and the Frogs pulled out one of the most exciting wins in history, 51-50. "I'm still surprised to see how calm and poised he was when we go back and watch the tape," senior offensive tackle Michael Toudouze said about Ballard's performance.

HORNED FROGS

But Ballard wasn't finished. He led the Frogs to nine straight wins, including a whipping of Iowa State in the Houston Bowl, and to the championship of the Mountain West Conference. It was the Horned Frogs' first conference title since they won the Southwest Conference in 1958.

"In truth," wrote Rick Waters, this unknown player who had no expectations for 2005 "saved the Frogs' season."

The blind date your friend promised would look like Brad Pitt or Jennifer Aniston but resembled a Munster or Cousin Itt. Your vacation that went downhill after the lost luggage. Often your expectations are raised only to be dashed. Sometimes it's best not to get your hopes up; then at least you have the possibility of being surprised.

Worst of all, perhaps, is when you realize that you are the one not meeting others' expectations. The fact is, though, that you aren't here to live up to what others think of you. Jesus didn't; in part, that's why they killed him. But he did meet God's expectations for his life, which was all that really mattered.

Because God's kingdom is so great, God does have great expectations for any who would enter, and you should not take them lightly. What the world expects from you is of no importance; what God expects from you is paramount.

I didn't expect this season to turn out the way it did. Not in a million years.
-- Jeff Ballard on the 2005 TCU football season

You have little if anything to gain from meeting the world's expectations of you; you have all of eternity to gain from meeting God's.

THE LEADER

Read Matthew 16:18-23.

"You are Peter, and on this rock I will build my church, and the gates of Hades will not overcome it" (v. 18).

The tough times his family endured when he was growing up helped mold Kenny Cain into a leader for the Horned Frogs.

Linebacker Cain was All-Big 12 as a senior in 2012. His last two seasons he led the Frogs in tackles. When he intercepted two passes against Virginia in the 2012 game, he became the first TCU linebacker with a pair of thefts since Chad Bayer in 1999.

Cain brought more than physical talent to the game. He was unquestionably the defense's inspirational leader on and off the field in 2012. His leadership skills were forged as he grew up, shaped by his strong family bonds in times of trouble.

In August 2005, Hurricane Katrina swept through the Cain home as he was about to start his freshman year of high school. "The floors were all flooded and there was wind damage," Cain recalled. "We got a lot of blankets and stuff and put them on the ground so we could sleep on them." With no power, the family relied on a generator brought over by an aunt. At night, they slept with the windows open, which let the mosquitoes in.

When the authorities forced the family from their home, Cain bounced around among relatives. He made it back to his high school only because he lived with one of his coaches for four years while he played football.

HORNED FROGS

What Cain remembered most about the calamity was how his own family stood tall and strong. "You could have been selfish," he said. "I love how my whole family stuck together."

Cain brought that sense of family togetherness with him to TCU. It was, in fact, the school's family atmosphere that lured him to Fort Worth. "I loved how all the players got along and how they interacted," he said. Like one big family, even in the tough times.

Every aspect of life that involves people – every organization, every group, every project, every team -- must have a leader. If goals are to be reached, somebody must take charge.

Even the early Christian church was no different. Jesus knew this, so he designated the leader in Simon Peter, who was such an unlikely choice to assume this awesome, world-changing responsibility that Jesus soon after rebuked him as "Satan."

In *Twelve Ordinary Men*, John MacArthur described Simon as "ambivalent, vacillating, impulsive, unsubmissive." Hardly a man to inspire confidence in his leadership skills. Yet, according to MacArthur, Peter became "the greatest preacher among the apostles" and the "dominant figure" in the birth of the church.

The implication for your own life is both obvious and unsettling. You may think you lack the attributes necessary to make a good leader for Christ. But consider Simon Peter, an ordinary man who allowed Christ to rule his life and became the foundation upon which the Christian church was built.

Cain's teammates look to him for guidance and strength.
-- Writer Stefan Stevenson on the defense's leader

God's leaders are men and women
who allow Jesus to lead them.

STOP, THIEF!

Read Exodus 22:1-15.

"A thief must certainly make restitution" (v. 2b).

Louisiana Tech coaches denied it, but the head Frog was convinced they were stealing his team's defensive signals in the first half of the 2011 Poinsettia Bowl.

After several seasons as the giant-slaying underdog, TCU "nearly found out what life is like at the other end of the rock" when the Frogs took on the Bulldogs in San Diego on Dec. 21. One writer suggested that a program accustomed to Fiesta Bowls and Rose Bowls with its bags packed for the penthouse of the Big 12 may not have had its collective pulse raised by a date with an 8-4 team from the Western Athletic Conference.

Whatever the reason, the fired-up Bulldogs bit the Frogs in the first half. The game was tied 10-10 at halftime, but the 18th-ranked Frogs were outgained 266 yards to 144. Tech had 16 first downs to TCU's seven with the Frogs managing only 59 yards rushing.

That performance left head coach Gary Patterson convinced the Bulldogs were stealing TCU's defensive signals. His suspicions were raised by the presence of former TCU coach Stan Eggen on the Tech sideline. So he changed the signals at halftime.

Whether or not any hanky-panky was going on, Tech refused to go away. A TCU fumble set up an easy score, and the Bulldogs hit a 61-yard bomb to lead 24-17 in the third quarter.

After that, though, the game belonged to the determined Frogs as they wore Tech down behind running backs Ed Wesley and Waymon James. They tied the game with a grueling, crushing 18-play drive that took 9 minutes and 21 seconds. Luke Shivers scored from the 1. The defense forced a punt, and Casey Pachall hit junior wide receiver Skye Dawson with a 42-yard touchdown pass that was the game winner. 31-24, Frogs.

After the change in signals, TCU's defense held Tech to 94 total yards with only three first downs the last half.

Buckle up your seat belt. Wear a bicycle or motorcycle helmet. Use your pooper scooper to clean up after your dog. Don't walk on the grass. Picky ordinances, picky laws – in all their great abundance, they're an inescapable part of our modern lives.

When Moses came stumbling down Mt. Sinai after spending time as God's secretary, he brought with him a whole mess of laws and regulations, many of which undoubtedly seem picky to us today. What some of them provide, though, are practical examples of what, for God, is the basic principle underlying the theft of personal property: what is wrong must be made right.

While most of us today won't have to worry too much about the theft of livestock such as oxen, sheep, and donkeys, making what is wrong right remains a way of life for Christians. To get right with other people requires anything from restitution to apologies. To get right with God requires Jesus Christ.

If they have the same signals as 10 years ago, they're not doing their job.
-- A La. Tech spokesman refuting Gary Patterson's theft charge

To make right the wrong of stealing requires restitution; to make right our relationship with God requires Jesus Christ.

REVELATION

Read Isaiah 53.

"But he was pierced for our transgressions, he was crushed for our iniquities; the punishment that brought us peace was upon him, and by his wounds we are healed" (v. 5).

Maybe TCU senior Hank Thorns had a little bit of the prophet in him when he tweeted before a game that he had never experienced fans storming the court in college.

Thorns had a remarkable two-year run at TCU from 2010-12 after transferring from Virginia Tech. A point guard, he finished sixth on TCU's all-time assists list. He was First-Team All-Mountain West his senior season.

Thorns did not exactly choose the most opportune time to post his wistful tweet. The Frogs' opposition on that evening of Feb. 14, 2012, was 11th-ranked UNLV. Apparently inspired by his own wish, though, Thorns went out against the Rebs and made it come true with "a sizzling, singular performance." The result was one of "the most electrifying wins in recent TCU history."

For most of the game, however, a storming of the court by jubilant TCU fans didn't appear to be on the agenda. The Rebels led at halftime and upped the lead to 18 points with 13:48 left to play.

But Thorns and the Frogs got hot and outscored UNLV 35-17 in the final 13 minutes. Thorns nailed two 3-pointers less than 30 seconds apart to propel TCU into an 83-83 tie with less than 3 minutes left. Sophomore forward Amric Fields sent the game into overtime at 85-85 with a steal and a drive down the lane.

Thorns' driving layup started the OT and he didn't let up. He scored eight in the extra period and finished with a career-high 32 points. TCU pulled off the 102-97 upset.

When the buzzer sounded, Thorns jumped on the press table, raised his arms, and shouted in exultation. When he jumped back down, he was swarmed by the TCU fans who had stormed the court -- just as he had spoken of hours before.

In our jaded age, we have relegated prophecy to dark rooms in which mysterious women peer into crystal balls or clasp our sweaty palms while uttering some vague generalities. At best, we understand a prophet as someone who predicts future events.

Within the pages of the Bible, though, we encounter something radically different. A prophet is a messenger from God, one who relays divine revelation to others.

Prophets seem somewhat foreign to us because in one very real sense the age of prophecy is over. In the name of Jesus, we have access to God through our prayers and through scripture. In searching for God's will for our lives, we seek divine revelation. We may speak only for ourselves and not for the greater body of Christ, but we do not need a prophet to discern what God would have us do. We need faith in the one whose birth, life, and death fulfilled more than 300 Bible prophecies.

I was hot; I can't explain it. I was feeling it.
-- Hank Thorns on his game that led to fans' storming the court

Persons of faith continuously seek
a word from God for their lives.

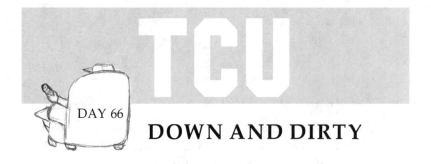

DOWN AND DIRTY

Read Isaiah 1:15-20.

"Though your sins are like scarlet, they shall be as white as snow; though they are red as crimson, they shall be like wool" (v. 18).

The Horned Frogs played "as glorious a game as ever a TCU team turned in" and won the 1935 national title as a result. It was glorious, but it sure wasn't pretty. What it was, was muddy.

Heavy rains for three days prior to the 1936 Sugar Bowl in New Orleans rendered the field "soggy and slippery," before the game began -- and it only got worse. More rain started falling at halftime, turning the gridiron into a "veritable morass."

Under those circumstances, TCU and LSU, the champions of the SEC, could well have let the conditions get the best of them. They didn't though. Despite the mud and a cold wind that "swept the rain in slanting sheets across the field," the teams played with spirit and intensity. They just didn't score much.

LSU's only score resulted from a Frog mistake. In the second period, junior quarterback Sammy Baugh, completing the first of his two All-American seasons, stepped on the end-zone line as he evaded a hard Tiger rush. The safety gave LSU a 2-0 lead.

Tight end Walter Roach, the first three-time All-Southwest Conference player in program history, booted the ensuing free kick to the LSU 40. In the rain and the mud, LSU fumbled, and end Willie Walls recovered for the Frogs.

HORNED FROGS

After a completed pass, TCU stalled. Despite the awful conditions, center Jack Tittle snapped the wet, slick, heavy ball perfectly to Baugh, who set it down for Taldon Manton's 36-yard field goal.

The rain worsened and the mud deepened in the last half, and the 3-2 score held up. When SMU lost to Stanford in the Rose Bowl, the 12-1 Horned Frogs were national champions.

Maybe you've never slopped any pigs and thus have never traipsed around a "hog wallow." You may not be a fan of mud boggin'. Still, you've worked on your car, planted a garden, played touch football in the rain, or endured some military training. You've been dirty.

Dirt, grime, and mud aren't the only sources of stains, however. We can also get dirty spiritually by not living in accordance with God's commands, by doing what's wrong, or by not doing what's right. We all experience temporary shortcomings and failures; we all slip and fall into the mud.

Whether we stay there or not, though, is a function of our relationship with Jesus. For the followers of Jesus, sin is not a way of life; it's an abnormality, so we don't stay in the filth. We seek a spiritual bath by expressing regret and asking for God's pardon in Jesus' name. God responds by washing our soul white as snow with his forgiveness.

Ordinarily, mud battles are dull shoving contests, but that was not the case in this Sugar Bowl scrap.
-- Writer Flem Hall on the '36 Sugar Bowl

**When your soul gets dirty, a powerful and
thorough cleansing agent is available
for the asking: God's forgiveness.**

DAY 67

PROVE IT!

Read Matthew 3.

"But John tried to deter him, saying, 'I need to be baptized by you, and do you come to me?'" (v. 14)

The Horned Frogs had to prove they belonged in a bowl game.

Head coach Dennis Franchione's first TCU team finished 6-5 in 1998. They beat only one squad with a winning record, handing Air Force its lone loss of the season. Those five losses were deceptive, however, as only one of them was by more than seven points.

When TCU received an invitation to the Sun Bowl while Utah, Colorado State, and Wyoming with their better records all stayed at home for the holidays, the critics started howling. They asserted TCU had no business playing a bowl game and would be blown off the field by its opponent, 8-4 Southern California. The Trojans were established as 16-point favorites over the disrespected Frogs.

So, clearly, the team had a lot to prove in El Paso on Dec. 31. It did just that. When the game was over, it was Southern Cal and the so-called experts -- and not the Horned Frogs -- who were embarrassed. TCU dominated the line of scrimmage, took control of the game early, led 28-3 in the third quarter, and then refused to let the Trojans rally in the 28-19 win.

Led by Basil Mitchell's 185 yards, TCU rushed for 314 yards and held the Trojans to -23 yards rushing, the worst performance in Southern Cal's history. Mitchell began the scoring with a 3-yard run in the first quarter and then scampered 60 yards three minutes later for another touchdown. When quarterback Patrick Batteaux scored on an 8-yard run, TCU led 21-0 just 5 1/2 minutes into the second quarter. Southern Cal was toast.

"We did believe," Franchione said. Few folks outside the team and its most loyal fans did, though -- until the Frogs proved their critics wrong.

You, too, have to prove yourself over and over again in your life. To your teachers, to that guy you'd like to date, to your parents, to your bosses, to the loan officer. It's always the same question: "Am I good enough?" Practically everything we do in life is aimed at proving that we are.

And yet, when it comes down to the most crucial situation in our lives, the answer is always a decisive and resounding "No!" Are we good enough to measure up to God? To deserve our salvation? John the Baptist knew he wasn't, and he was not only Jesus' relative but God's hand-chosen prophet. If he wasn't good enough, what chance do we have?

The notion that only "good" people can be church members is a perversion of Jesus' entire ministry. Nobody is good enough – without Jesus. Everybody is good enough – with Jesus. That's not because of anything we have done for God, but because of what he has done for us. We have nothing to prove to God.

We might have been the only ones in the nation, but we believed we could beat [the Trojans].
                                    -- Dennis Franchione on the 1998 Sun Bowl

The bad news is we can't prove to God's satisfaction how good we are; the good news is that because of Jesus we don't have to.

ZINGERS

Read Luke 20:9-19.

"The teachers of the law and the chief priests looked for a way to arrest him immediately, because they knew he had spoken this parable against them" (v. 19).

A touchdown that really wasn't led to an insult that really was.

Texas was 8-0 and ranked No. 1 when the Frogs, who would finish 3-5-2, hopped into Memorial Stadium on Nov. 18, 1961. The afternoon was a frustrating one for the big cows. Sophomore linebacker Tommy Crutcher, who would be an All-American fullback as a senior, stopped a Texas runner at the 1-yard line on the Horns' opening possession. After that, the determined TCU defense held Texas five more times inside the Frog 30.

In the second quarter at midfield, quarterback Sonny Gibbs pitched the ball to halfback Larry Thomas, who then handed it back to Gibbs. He wound up and "threw the heck out of it." The ball found right end Buddy Iles, a future TCU hall-of-famer, at the 8-yard line. A Texas player made a desperate diving tackle, and according to Gibbs, "Buddy actually landed on the 2 and bounced over the goal line." To the Horns' dismay, the refs awarded TCU a touchdown, the only one of the game. TCU pulled off one of the greatest upsets in its history, 6-0.

After the game, a disgruntled Darrell Royal, the Texas head coach, insulted all things TCU when he referred to the Frogs as the "cockroaches." He spent years trying to refute the remark, declaring repeatedly, "I never called these people cockroaches. I said they were like a bunch of cockroaches." Actually, Royal's full statement was a bit more clever. The Frogs were like cockroaches, he said, because "it's not so much what they eat and carry off; it's what they fall into and mess up." Like his team's national title hopes.

There's nothing like a ripping good insult to rile us up as Darrell Royal's words did to TCU players and fans in 1961. We take an insult exactly as it is meant: personally.

Few people throughout history can match Jesus, of all people, for delivering a well-placed zinger, and few insults throughout history can match the one he tossed at the religious authorities in Luke 20. Jesus' remarks were so accurate and so severe that the targets of his insult responded by seeking to have him arrested.

Using a vineyard as the centerpiece of an extensive allegory, Jesus insulted the priests and their lackeys by declaring that they had insulted God in rejecting his rule over them. They had sought to own God's kingdom for themselves.

They were truly just a bunch of hypocrites. But before we get too smug, we need to take a good look around. Little has changed. We still seek to live our lives on our terms, not God's. The world is in such a mess because we want to run God's vineyard, instead of surrendering to him. Jesus delivered that insult right at us.

I've tried to tell him that his version is the same as calling someone a cockroach, but he doesn't see it that way.
-- Buddy Iles on friend Darrell Royal's cockroach insult

In insulting the priests for rebelling against God, Jesus delivered a zinger right at us.

RECIPE FOR DISASTER

Read Luke 21:5-11, 25-28.

"There will be great earthquakes, famines and pestilences in various places, and fearful events and great signs from heaven" (v. 11).

The Frogs fell victim to the most disastrous ninth inning in the history of the program -- perhaps in all of college baseball -- but still were able to come back and win.

Less than a week before they met on May 24, 2012, TCU and the San Diego State Aztecs had played a nice, sane 3-0 game. This rematch featured more offense than that, but it, too, was a pretty typical baseball game -- until the ninth inning. What happened then led TCU head baseball coach Jim Schlossnagle to exclaim, "Baseball is crazy."

What happened -- first of all -- was the biggest meltdown in TCU diamond history. "A Frogs victory was considered a foregone conclusion" with only three outs to get and a big 14-4 lead. Then came an unmitigated disaster.

Eight hits, including two home runs, a number of wild pitches, a hit batsman, and an error combined to produce 11 Aztec runs. It could have been worse. The Frogs had managed to get only one out during all that time. Stefan Crichton, the fourth pitcher of the inning, got a strikeout and a flyout to finally end the carnage.

"It just kept getting closer and closer, and [it] seemed like we just didn't have enough runs to keep it out of [their] grasp," said

TCU infielder Jantzen Witte, the 2013 Big 12 Co-Student Athlete of the Year. Indeed, there weren't enough runs; the Frogs trailed 15-14 as they came to bat in the bottom of the ninth.

Junior Kyle Von Tungeln slammed a one-out home run for the tie. A single, a double, and a walk loaded the bases in front of a single from Brett Johnson that chased catcher Davy Wright home with the winning run. TCU had avoided a disastrous loss.

Admittedly, TCU's suffering an 11-run ninth inning is insignificant as true disasters go. That's because we live in a world that seems to be either struck by one disaster after another or is the home of several ongoing and seemingly permanent disasters. Earthquakes virtually obliterate an entire nation; children around the world starve to death every day. Floods devastate cities and shatter lives; oil pollutes our oceans and seashores. Can we even count the number of wars that are going on at any one time?

This apparently unending litany of disaster is enough to make us all give up hope. Maybe – but not for the followers of Jesus Christ. The truth is that Jesus' disciples should find reassurance of their ultimate hope in the world's constant disasters because this is exactly what Jesus said would happen.

These disasters indicate that the time of our redemption is drawing near. How near is up to God to decide. Nevertheless, this is a season of hope and great promise for those of the faith.

That's the most ridiculous game I've ever been part of.
-- Jantzen Witte on the win over San Diego State

**Jesus told us what to do when disaster threatens
to overwhelm us and our world:
'Stand up and lift up your heads.'**

DAY 70

DRY RUN

Read John 4:1-15.

*"Everyone who drinks this water will be thirsty again,
but whoever drinks the water I give him will never thirst.
Indeed, the water I give him will become in him a spring
of water welling up to eternal life" (vv. 13-14).*

For the Horned Frogs, the drought stretched across 35 years. A drive for the ages ended it.

On Nov. 25, 1994, TCU took the field with a chance to accomplish something the program had not done since 1959: win at least a share of the football championship of the Southwest Conference. The opponent, the Red Raiders of Texas Tech, could claim the title outright with a win in the nationally televised game.

Junior quarterback Max Knake hit senior receiver Jimmy Oliver, the team's fastest player, with an 89-yard bomb in the second quarter and with a 62-yard strike in the fourth quarter to give the Frogs a 16-14 lead. Knake was the league's co-offensive Player of the Year in 1994 on his way to setting TCU career records for completions, passing yards, and touchdowns, all subsequently broken by Andy Dalton.

The Red Raiders seemed to have saved themselves, though, when they kicked a 41-yard field goal with only 6:23 to play for a 17-16 lead. After the kickoff, the Frogs set up shop at their own 31. Knake told his offensive line, "This is up to you guys. If you open the holes, Andre will get us there." Andre was tailback Andre

Davis, who entered the game as the nation's fourth-leading rusher. "I kind of knew it was going to fall on my shoulders," Davis said.

The line responded and so did Davis. The result was one of the greatest and most memorable drives in TCU football history.

Davis went for 12 and 28. On third-and-6 from the Tech 23, he ripped off a 14-yard draw. Two plays later from the 6, Davis scored on another draw with 3:59 to play. For good measure, he added the two-point conversion. The drought was over: 24-17, TCU.

You can walk across that river you boated on in the spring. The city's put all neighborhoods on water restriction. That beautiful lawn you fertilized and seeded will turn a sickly, pale green and may lapse all the way to brown. Somebody wrote "Wash Me" on the rear window of your truck.

The sun bakes everything, including the concrete. The earth itself seems exhausted, just barely hanging on. It's a drought.

It's the way a soul that shuts God out looks.

God instilled the physical sensation of thirst in us to warn us of our body's need for water. He also gave us a spiritual thirst that can be quenched only by his presence in our lives. Without God, we are like tumbleweeds, dried out and windblown, offering the illusion of life where there is only death.

Living water – water of life – is readily available in Jesus. We may drink our fill, and thus we slake our thirst and end our soul's drought – forever.

They needed something they could take with them for the rest of their lives, and now they've got it.
-- TCU head coach Pat Sullivan on the Frogs' drought-ending win

Our soul thirsts for God's refreshing presence.

STORY TIME

Read Luke 8:26-39.

"'Return home and tell how much God has done for you.'
So the man went away and told all over town how much
Jesus had done for him" (v. 39).

Jim Swink had some stories to tell about life as a Horned Frog.

Swink led TCU to a pair of Southwest-Conference titles as an All-American running back in 1955 and 1956. He led the nation in scoring as a junior in 1955 and was second in the nation in rushing. He finished second in the vote for the Heisman Trophy. He was inducted into the College Football Hall of Fame in 1980.

Swink was recruited to TCU even though the coaches never saw him play football. Not until the basketball season did assistant coach Allie White get a chance to see him play. "On the basis of the way he moved on the court, I told [head coach] Abe [Martin] we ought to get him," White said.

By the time the Baylor game rolled around in 1955, "the team's confidence in Swink bordered on cockiness" as a story from that game illustrates. All-Southwest Conference guard Vernon Uecker recalled that in the game the Frogs sat on their own 1-yard line "with about third-and-25 and Ray Taylor came in" and told quarterback Chuck Curtis, "Abe says punt." Curtis asked, "Did he say when?" Taylor said no. So Curtis called a running play to Swink, and he picked up the first down. After another play, he gave the ball to Swink again, and he went 65 yards for a touchdown. The Frogs covered 99 yards in three plays and scored.

Uecker also had a Swink story to tell from the battle for the Cotton Bowl against Texas in '55. (See Devotion No. 55.) Swink broke off a 62-yard scoring run behind a block from end Bryan Engram. He "zigged back to the right, zagged back left" and left his own blockers -- all-conference tackle Don Cooper and Uecker -- "lying on the turf." "We decided to just stay there" and watch, Uecker laughed. "We couldn't keep up with him, anyway."

So you don't have football stories to relate as Jim Swink and his teammates did. You nevertheless have a story to tell; it's the story of your life and it's unique. No one else among the billions of people on this planet can tell the same story.

Part of that story is your encounter with Jesus. It's the most important chapter of all, but, strangely enough, believers in Jesus Christ often don't tell it. Otherwise brave and daring Christian men and women who wouldn't think twice of skydiving or white-water rafting often quail when they are faced with the prospect of speaking about Jesus to someone else. It's the dreaded "W" word: witness. "I just don't know what to say," they sputter.

But witnessing is nothing but telling your story. No one can refute it; no one can claim it isn't true. You don't get into some great theological debate for which you're ill prepared. You just tell the beautiful, awesome story of Jesus and you.

To succeed in your sport or your life, you have to go out and write your own story.
-- Motivational-Quotes-for-Athletes.com

We all have a story to tell, but the most important part of all is the chapter where we meet Jesus.

NAME DROPPING

Read Exodus 3:13-20.

*"God said to Moses, 'I AM WHO I AM. This is what
you are to say to the Israelites: 'I AM has sent me to you'"
(v. 14).*

It took twelve years for the family of Ricky Carder, Jr., to dis-
cover how appropriate his nickname really was.

His folks dubbed their newest baby "Tank" when he weighed
33 pounds only eighteen months after his birth. Tank Carder, of
course, is a TCU legend, a two-time All-American linebacker who
made perhaps the most famous play in recent Frog history by
swatting away Wisconsin's try for the two-point conversion, thus
preserving the win in the 2011 Rose Bowl. (See Devotion No. 16.)

Ricky was 13 when he was nearly killed in a one-car accident.
He suffered a broken back, a collapsed lung, a punctured dia-
phragm, and internal bleeding. He survived at all because he in-
stinctively held onto the window frame of the car as it flipped
several times and struck a tree.

"That car looked like a crumpled-up piece of aluminum foil,"
said Tank's mother, Marti. On the scene as he struggled to breathe,
Tank told his mother he didn't want to die. She told him, "Tank,
pray to God, baby, because it's in God's hands now." He did just
that as a helicopter carried him to a Houston trauma center.

For about 24 hours, whether Tank lived or not was uncertain.
His mother said the doctors called him "the miracle child because

he was so broken. . . . It was probably a week before we knew he was going to walk again."

Tank had a six-week hospital stay and wore a body brace for six more months. He wasn't cleared for sports until his sophomore year. After that, though, the rest is TCU history for the boy who survived blows that might well have stalled a tank

Nicknames such as "Tank" are not slapped haphazardly upon individuals but rather reflect widely held perceptions about the person named. Proper names can also have a particular physical or character trait associated with them.

Nowhere throughout the long march of history has this concept been more prevalent than in the Bible, where a name is not a mere label but is an expression of the essential nature of the named one. That is, a person's name reveals his or her character. Even God shares this concept; to know the name of God is to know God as he has chosen to reveal himself to us.

What does your name say about you? Honest, trustworthy, a seeker of the truth and a person of God? Or does the mention of your name cause your coworkers to whisper snide remarks, your neighbors to roll their eyes, or your friends to start making allowances for you?

Most importantly, what does your name say about you to God? He, too, knows you by name.

Tank has got more determination than anybody I've ever met.
-- Marti Carder on her son

Live so that your name evokes positive associations by people you know, by the public, and by God.

THE OUTER LIMITS

Read Genesis 18:1-15.

"Is anything too hard for the Lord?" (v. 14a)

When she finished her TCU career, Sandora Irvin was the greatest shot-blocker in women's college basketball history. That feat seemed almost inevitable; when she started playing the game, the only thing she could do was block shots.

To declare Irvin the greatest women's player in TCU history is perhaps to do little more than state the obvious. She was first-team All-America as a senior in 2005. She set the NCAA record for blocks in a game with 16 and blocks in a career with 480 (the latter since broken). She still holds numerous TCU records, including field goals made, free throws made, points, scoring average, rebounds, and the obvious blocked shots.

Irvin started out, though, as a player with extremely limited skills. When she was in the second grade, she moved in with her grandmother, who was loving but strict. Grades came first. No playing outside after school. One day when she was in the sixth grade, Irvin wistfully looked across the street at a group of boys playing basketball in a park. Daringly, she broke the rules and ran outside to join them.

She had never played the game, and besides, she was a girl. No boy would choose her for his team. After all, she couldn't dribble, she couldn't shoot, she couldn't pass. But she was taller than most of the boys and height is its own talent in basketball.

When she got into her first game, she blocked a shot. The boys roared, impressed. She came back every day after that, doing only what she could: blocking shots and falling in love with the game. Eventually, her grandmother found her out but let her play on her school's seventh-grade team. Irvin's teammates dubbed her "Tall But Nothin'" because all she could do was block shots.

Determined to improve her game, Irvin joined an AAU team that spring. History shows she did indeed get a whole lot better.

You've probably never tried any number of things you have dreamed about doing at one time or another. Like starting your own business. Going back to school. Campaigning for elected office. Playing organized basketball as Sandora Irvin did.

But what holds you back? Perhaps you hesitate because you see only your limitations, both those you've imposed on yourself and those of which others constantly remind you. Maybe, though, it's time to see yourself the way God does.

God sees you as you are and also as you can be. In God's eyes, your possibilities are limitless. The realization of those latent possibilities, however, depends upon your depending upon God for direction, guidance, and strength. While you may quail in the face of the challenge that lies before you, nothing is too hard for the Lord.

You can free yourself from that which blights your dreams by depending not on yourself but on God.

Dear Coach. I will improve my game. We will never lose again.
    -- Sandora Irvin in a letter to her junior high coach after a loss

Pray like everything depends upon God;
work like everything depends upon you.

BROKEN DREAMS

Read Joel 2:28-32.

"I will pour out my Spirit on all people. . . . Your old men will dream dreams" (v. 28).

Because of the great football teams Dutch Meyer built at TCU in the 1930's, Fort Worth became a star on the nation's road map instead of an insignificant red dot." But Meyer never realized one of his biggest dreams.

Meyer coached the Frogs for nineteen seasons (1934-52) and won 109 games, second all-time only to Gary Patterson. His teams won two national titles and three Southwest Conference championships. He won two Sugar Bowls and a Cotton Bowl and coached a Heisman Trophy winner in Davey O'Brien. He was inducted into the College Football Hall of Fame in 1956.

Despite all that success, one of Meyer's dreams -- "the most cherished sports prize of all in the 1930s" -- eluded him. The dream was an appearance in the Rose Bowl. He came close twice.

In 1935, unbeaten TCU and SMU met with the winner getting the bid to Pasadena. SMU won a thriller from Sammy Baugh and the Frogs 20-14. "I just laid my head down in the press box and cried," said J. Williard Ridings, TCU's sports information director.

Meyer had his best chance at the Rose Bowl in 1938 when his team finished No. 1 in the rankings. In those days, the host team could pick its opponent, and Southern Cal chose Duke instead of TCU. In New York for O'Brien's Heisman Trophy presentation,

HORNED FROGS

Meyer fired a salvo at the Trojans. Without exactly saying so, he accused them of ducking TCU and its awesome offense. "They took a team that scored less points in a season than we did in one game," he growled.

Flem Hall of *The Star-Telegram* wrote that not getting the bid wasn't all that bad because it left the Frogs something to shoot for in future seasons. But Meyer's team never lost fewer than three games in a season after 1938, and he never got another shot at realizing his dream of the Rose Bowl.

Like Dutch Meyer, we all have particular dreams. Perhaps to make a million dollars, write the Great American Novel, or find the perfect spouse. More likely than not, though, we gradually lose our hold on those dreams. They slip away from us as we surrender them to the reality of everyday living.

But we also have general dreams. For world peace. For an end to hunger. That no child should ever again be afraid. These dreams we hold onto doggedly, as if something inside us insists that even though the world gets itself into a bigger mess every year, one day everything will be all right.

That's because it will be. God has promised a time when his spirit will rule the world. Jesus spoke of a time when he will return to claim his kingdom. In that day, our dreams of peace and plenty and the banishment of hate and want will become reality.

Our dreams based on God's promises will come true.

To achieve in sports you first have to have a dream, and then you must act on that dream.
-- Speed skater Dianne Holum

Dreams based on God's promises will come true.

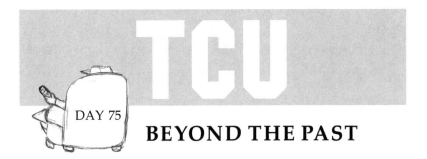

DAY 75

BEYOND THE PAST

Read Colossians 3:1-10.

*"You used to walk in these ways, in the life you once lived.
But now you must rid yourself of all such things" (vv. 7,
8a).*

In a time long past, the TCU football coach had tenure like an
English professor and didn't want a big staff of assistants.

Othol Hershel "Abe" Martin was the head football coach at
TCU from 1953-1966, compiling a 74-64-7 record and winning
three Southwest Conference championships. In a time before football coaches were expected to present a carefully groomed and
polished image to the media and had their schedules carefully set,
Martin himself welcomed visitors to his office. He was "a down-
to-earth guy in a rumpled suit, the stub of a cigar in his mouth,
his hat pulled over his forehead, his eyes peering over spectacles .
. . and his feet propped unceremoniously upon the desk."

In a time before coaches' salaries escalated into seven digits,
Martin made about $14,500 a year late in his career. He quaintly
declared that his job wasn't all about winning games, that he
was "building character" and "I don't see how you can find any
grounds for having football if that isn't its purpose."

In a time before athletic departments separated themselves
from the university, the trustees awarded Martin faculty tenure
after his third season at the helm. "I think athletic personnel
should be treated the same insofar as security is concerned as

members of the English department," declared the school's chancellor. Funds raised by the booster organization were administered by the school's business office, not the athletic department.

In a time before coaching staffs were bloated, for much of his career Martin refused to hire more than three assistants and one freshman coach. "I like to coach kids," he said, "but I'd hate to have to coach a bunch of coaches."

The past often seems quaint to us as illustrated by TCU's football program back in the days decades ago when Abe Martin was the head Frog.

But in our personal lives, the past usually isn't quaint at all. Instead, it often haunts us like a ghost. We lug around our regrets and memories of our past failures, omissions, and shortcomings, donning them each day as we do our clothes.

Short of utter callousness and severe memory problems, only one way exists to free ourselves totally from the past: the change offered through salvation in Jesus Christ. Even when we fall on our knees in despair and cry out to Jesus, we sometimes falsely believe that salvation and forgiveness can never be ours. That's because many desperate seekers fall prey to the fallacy that they must be perfect before Jesus will accept them. The truth is that we need Jesus because we are not perfect.

Jesus didn't die for our past but for our future. He died to free us from the past and to replace it with a glorious future.

[TCU] has the most sensible approach to athletics of any in the major-college field.

-- Paul Ridings, Frog Club officer in the 1960s

Every saint has a past; every sinner has a future.

TOOLS OF THE TRADE

Read Ephesians 6:10-18.

"Put on the full armor of God so that you can take your stand against the devil's schemes" (v. 11).

What Joe Brown needed was the right tool.

In the spring of 2008, Brown's senior season at TCU wasn't going the way that either he or his coach, John Kenneson, had expected. The school's star javelin thrower had worked extremely hard to perfect his technique, and he had the arm strength the sport required. "He was doing a lot correctly," Kenneson said, "but he was not getting the results we thought he ought to."

So they tinkered and tweaked, but the javelin still wasn't flying as far as they thought it should. Eventually, Kenneson fell back on one of the time-proven truisms of track: An athlete is only as good as his equipment. With javelins rated in calibers according to the stiffness of the shaft, Kenneson decided Brown needed to step up from the 60-meter javelin he was using.

TCU didn't have one on hand, so Kenneson contacted an All-American thrower and two-time Olympian he had coached and explained the problem. "I know exactly what you need," he said. "It's in my garage. I'll send it to you." What he sent was a 90-meter javelin, the highest rated tool Brown could use.

The results were spectacular. Brown immediately gained more than five feet on his throws, "a giant leap in a sport in which inches separate good from great." He won the Mountain West

HORNED FROGS

Conference title on his first throw, TCU's first javelin championship since Wes Ritchey captured the Southwest Conference title
in 1954. Brown set a school record at the Midwest Regional and
thus for the first time was heading for the NCAA Championships.
He was named TCU's first-ever All-American in the javelin and
later was the first Horned Frog to be named the Mountain West
Conference Male Student-Athlete of the Year.

Like Joe Brown, we all need the right tools to excel. How many
times have we or a co-worker fussed at the office about not having
all we need to do the job right? Just try pulling off some minor
car repairs or assembling the kids' new trampoline with only a
hammer. We need tools.

That applies to our faith life also. Christians are under attack,
not just in countries ruled by despots but in America. The assaults
are a sure sign we're doing something right for God and the devil
isn't happy about it.

But we need tools to fight off the attacks. Ever dependable, ever
thinking of us, God has given those tools to us in abundance.
Collectively, they are the armor of God. Individually, they are the
truth we proclaim, the righteousness of our cause, the peace in
our hearts, the strength of our faith, the surety of our salvation,
and the power of both the Word of God and of our prayers.

They are the tools we need to win the battle against the enemies
of our Lord, but we must use them or they are to no avail.

If you know how to use it, a superior javelin will reward you.
-- TCU track and field associate coach John Kenneson

God has provided us with the tools we need to
win the battle against the spiritual forces of evil.

FAMILY TIES

Read Mark 3:31-35.

*"[Jesus] said, 'Here are my mother and my brothers!
Whoever does God's will is my brother and sister and
mother'" (vv. 34-35).*

A deceased family member helped shape Reggie Hunt's life.

Hunt grew up with his younger brother and his mother. "My mom and my brother are my best friends," he said. "We struggled money-wise, but as far as love, we had plenty."

Also a big part of the family was a cousin, Fred Washington, ten years Hunt's senior who served as a role model and surrogate father. Washington was a four-year letterman at defensive tackle for the Horned Frogs from 1986-1989. He was a co-captain as a senior and was drafted by the Chicago Bears in 1990. Washington introduced Hunt to football as the "quiet, resident coach [of] a ragtag team of teenagers who played street football at Hunt's grandmother's home during the holidays."

On Dec. 21, 1990, the Hunt family got a phone call that changed Reggie's life. Washington had been killed in a car wreck. "He was my inspiration," Hunt said. "I felt like I was next, and I was the only one who could take his place." Thus, the 13-year-old, who had concentrated on track in junior high, switched to football.

Hunt was a high-school All-America at running back and was All-State at defensive back. When it came time to choose a college, he picked TCU because that was where Washington had played.

Hunt was a starter at running back as a freshman in 1996 and as a sophomore until the fifth game. Injuries had devastated the secondary, and the coaches moved him across the line to safety.

Hunt starred on defense, earning second-team All-WAC honors in 1998 and '99. He set a TCU record as a senior by averaging 34.1 yards per kickoff return. All the while, he played with a tattoo on his arm to remind him of Fred Washington and that he was "following in [his cousin's] unfinished footsteps."

Some wit said families are like fudge, mostly sweet with a few nuts. You can probably call the names of your sweetest relatives, whom you cherish as Reggie Hunt did Fred Washington, and of the nutty ones too, whom you try to avoid at a family reunion.

Like it or not, you have a family, and that's God's doing. God cherishes the family so much that he chose to live in one as a son, a brother, and a cousin.

One of Jesus' more startling actions was to redefine the family. No longer is it a single household of blood relatives or even a clan or a tribe. Jesus' family is the result not of an accident of birth but rather a conscious choice. All those who do God's will are members of Jesus' family.

What a startling and downright wonderful thought! You have family members out there you don't even know who stand ready to love you just because you're part of God's family.

[Reggie] Hunt's arm says it all, in black letters, a tattoo across the width of his bicep: F.E.W. And then below it: 1967-1990.
-- The TCU Magazine

**For followers of Jesus, family comes not from
a shared ancestry but from a shared faith.**

THE CHALLENGE

Read Matthew 4:12-25.

"Come, follow me," Jesus said (v. 19).

Raymond "Rags" Matthews often issued personal challenges to the teams he played against, and once in a big game he delivered the challenge by walking right into the opposition's huddle.

Matthews enrolled briefly at Texas A&M before he called TCU head coach Matty Bell to come get him because he had discovered that the school "was out in the middle of a prairie and there were no women." The coach did as he was told and never regretted it.

Matthews was TCU's first All-America, an end who was "a good receiver and an absolute terror on defense." He was All-Southwest Conference in 1926 and '27 and received All-America nods in 1927.

A bona fide trash talker, Matthews' gall perhaps reached its zenith in 1927 against the undefeated Aggies. Late in the game, which ended in a scoreless tie, the A&M huddle was rudely interrupted by a strange voice asking, "Y'all got the guts to run my way?" The players suddenly realized they had a true twelfth man in their huddle; it was Matthews.

The challenge came just when the Frogs needed some inspiration. They had gamely battled the favored Aggies all afternoon, but now A&M sat with a first down on the TCU 2-yard line. That's when Matthews took his little hike and spoke his little piece. The Aggies foolishly accepted his challenge.

On first down, they sent their three-time All-SWC back right at

Matthews. No gain. On second down, he batted down a pass. On third down, they came at him again. No gain.

Matthews then stepped across the line again and repeated his challenge. The A&M running back insulted Matthews' mama and then issued his own challenge: "Get ready. Here I come." He came but Matthews was ready. After the play and Matthews' tackle, the ball was still on the 2.

Like TCU's athletic teams every time they take the field or the court, we are challenged daily. Life is a testing ground; God intentionally set it up that way. If we are to grow in character, confidence, and perseverance, and if we are to make a difference in the world, we must meet challenges head-on. Few things in life are as boring and as destructive to our sense of self-worth as a job that doesn't offer any challenges.

Our faith life is the same way. The moment we answered Jesus' call to "Come, follow me," we took on the most difficult challenge we will ever face. We are called to be holy by walking in Jesus' footsteps in a world that seeks to render our Lord irrelevant and his influence negligible. The challenge Jesus places before us is to put our faith and our trust in him and not in ourselves or the transitory values of the secular world.

Daily walking in Jesus' footsteps is a challenge, but the path takes us all the way right up to the gates of Heaven – and then right on through.

I always did some talking out on the field.

-- Raymond Matthews

To accept Jesus as Lord is to joyfully take on the challenge of living a holy life in an unholy world.

THE CHALLENGE   159

YOURS TO COMMAND

Read Exodus 20:1-17.

*"God spoke all these words: 'I am the Lord your God . . . .
You shall have no other gods before me'" (vv. 1, 3).*

Gary Patterson issued one terse command to his team at halftime: Play like what you are. They obeyed.

The Horned Frogs of 2010 were ranked fifth in the nation on Oct. 2 when they took on Colorado State at Fort Collins in their Mountain West opener. The Rams were only 1-3 on their way to a long 3-9 season, so the Frogs were heavily favored.

Nobody apparently told the Rams they weren't even supposed to show up for this one. The TCU offense struggled in the first half, hurting its own case with several mistakes. For instance, Andy Dalton's receivers dropped four passes on TCU's first possession, which meant the Frogs could manage only a 29-yard field goal from Ross Evans.

The offense put together another drive late in the first quarter but again had to call on Evans for a field goal that made it a 6-0 game. And that was it at halftime: no touchdowns and the lowest first-half output of the season for the offense.

Needless to say, the head coach was not too pleased. So just before the second-half kickoff, he gathered his offense about him and issued a command. "You're the No. 5 team in the nation," he said. "Play like it."

They did. The Frogs drove 80 yards in 2:20 to start the last half with Ed Wesley breaking off an 8-yard TD run. A 47-yard sprint by Matthew Tucker behind a block from fullback Luke Shivers set up the score. Later in the quarter, Wesley used a block from All-American tackle Marcus Cannon to score from the 3. Wide receiver Jimmy Young caught a 39-yard scoring toss from Dalton in the fourth quarter to finish the scoring.

The Frogs obeyed the command their leader had issued and won 27-0, rolling up a season-high 346 yards rushing.

If you've ever played any organized sports, been within shouting distance of the military, or held any steady job, then you've been issued commands you were expected to obey, often without comment. It's the way of the hierarchy. Moving up the proverbial ladder means you get to issue some of those commands.

That's even true in our spiritual life. At the top of that hierarchy is the ultimate authority -- God himself -- who has issued a list of his orders to us. We call them the Ten Commandments.

Rather than just instructions we are to obey blindly, God's commandments constitute a blueprint for how we are to act in our dealing with other people and with him. A life dedicated to Jesus is a life devoted to relationships, and God's commands emphasize that the social life and the spiritual life cannot be sundered.

God's relationship to you is one of unceasing, unqualified love, and you are to mirror that divine love in your relationships with others. God commands, we obey.

Society today treats the Ten Commandments as if they were the ten suggestions. Never compromise on right or wrong.
-- College baseball coach Gordie Gillespie

In love, God commands. In love, we obey.

DAY 80

AT A LOSS

Read Philippians 3:1-9.

"I consider everything a loss compared to the surpassing greatness of knowing Christ Jesus my Lord, for whose sake I have lost all things" (v. 8).

In every volleyball game she played for TCU, Kourtney Edwards bore a reminder of her loss.

Edwards was a redshirt freshman in 2006 when her mother, Marie Annette Johnson, died. Edwards admitted that her mom's death "shook up her life and left her career in doubt." The two had celebrated victories and agonized over defeats together. For Edwards, volleyball held little meaning without her mom.

Gradually, with the support of her teammates, their families, and her extended family, Edwards recaptured her love for volleyball again. One active step she took helped. Every game, Edwards printed the initials MAJ in block capital letters on her wrists. The temporary tattoo reminded her that her mother was "my strength and best friend, and I know she will always be there."

She ultimately decided to keep playing because she knew that was what her mother would have wanted. "One thing she always told me was that I made her proud," Edwards said. So she went back to volleyball "to keep making her proud."

She also made Frog fans very proud in 2009 as a senior star on the greatest team in TCU volleyball history. The squad went 26-6 in the regular season, the highest win total in program history, and earned the school's first-ever berth in the NCAA Tournament. They finished the season with 27 wins.

Edwards led the team in kills, blocks, and points and was All-Mountain West Conference, All-Region, and Honorable Mention All-America. She finished up as TCU's career record-holder in blocks and in the top ten in kills and points.

"I know [my mom would] be proud of what we've accomplished," she said in looking back. "I know that for sure."

Maybe, as it was with Kourtney Edwards, it was when a family member died. Perhaps it wasn't so staggeringly tragic: your dog died, your best friend moved away, or an older sibling left home. Sometime in your youth or early adult life, though, you learned that loss is a part of life.

Loss inevitably diminishes your life, but loss and the grief that accompanies it are part of the price of loving. When you first encountered loss, you learned that you were virtually helpless to prevent it or escape it.

There is life after loss, though, because you have one sure place to turn. Jesus can share your pain and ease your suffering, but he doesn't stop there. Through the loss of his own life, he has transformed death -- the ultimate loss -- into the ultimate gain of eternal life.

In Jesus lies the promise that one day loss itself will die.

I know she's watching me and cheering me on.
-- Kourtney Edwards on her mom

**Jesus not only eases the pain of our losses
but transforms the loss caused by death
into the gain of eternal life.**

UNEXPECTEDLY

Read Matthew 24:36-51.

"No one knows about that day or hour, not even the angels in heaven, nor the Son, but only the Father" (v. 36).

Jerry Hughes sure didn't expect that his TCU football career would turn out the way it did.

In the summer of 2006, Hughes arrived in Fort Worth for his first summer workouts. He had been a star in high school as a running back and a kick returner, and, with LaDainian Tomlinson as his inspiration, he expected more of the same at TCU.

The first sign that his expectations might not be met came quickly. The number on his practice jersey was 98. Hughes determined that the high numbers were assigned "to the guys who were going to be redshirted."

Then, however, he received a packet for players on the defensive line and was told to meet with coordinator Dick Bumpas. "I started thinking maybe my running back days are numbered," Hughes said.

His perception was dead on. Head coach Gary Patterson met with Hughes in his office and showed him video of defensive end Tommy Blake sacking a number of quarterbacks. Like Hughes, Blake had been an all-state running back; he had -- grudgingly as it were -- made the switch to defense at TCU after a redshirt season. *College Football News* named him its Mountain West Defensive Player of the Year in 2005.

Patterson told Hughes he would follow in Blake's footsteps by switching to defense. Hughes went along with the idea though he had some reservations. As he left the office, he thought, "I'm 200 pounds. How is this going to work?"

Pretty well. Hughes was a two-time All-America in 2008 and '09. As a senior in 2009, he won the Ted Hendricks Award as the country's best defensive end and the Lott Trophy for his personal character and his academic excellence.

Just like Jerry Hughes and his expectations of being a running back, we think we've got everything figured out and under control, and then something unexpected happens. About the only thing we can expect from life with any certainty is the unexpected.

God is that way too, suddenly showing up to remind us he's still around. A friend who calls and tells you he's praying for you, a hug from your child or grandchild, a lone lily that blooms in your yard -- unexpected moments when the divine comes crashing into our lives with such clarity that it takes our breath away and brings tears to our eyes.

But why shouldn't God do the unexpected? The only factor limiting what God can do in our lives is the paucity of our own faith. We should expect the unexpected from God, this same deity who caught everyone by surprise by unexpectedly coming to live among us as a man, and who will return when we least expect it.

All this is much more than we expected. We didn't see this coming at all.
– Jerry Hughes' mom, Pam, on his defensive success

God continually does the unexpected,
like showing up as Jesus,
who will return unexpectedly.

FEAR FACTOR

Read Matthew 14:22-33.

"[The disciples] cried out in fear. But Jesus immediately said to them: 'Take courage! It is I. Don't be afraid'" (vv. 26-27).

Fear is never an option for Eddie Williamson.

On Nov. 13, 2010, in the first quarter of the Frogs' 40-35 win over San Diego State, Williamson, the offensive line coach, started feeling some tension in his chest. "I thought I was just being emotional about senior day," he said.

But shortly thereafter, he knew it wasn't emotion. He had had CPR training, and he knew it was trouble. He calmly turned to co-offensive coordinator Jarrett Anderson and said, "I think I'm having a heart attack." He was. The team doctor escorted him to the locker room, and when his wife, Patty, came in, he asked her, "Did we score?"

TCU doctors immediately started monitoring the coach's vital signs, and he was soon taken by ambulance to a hospital. In the emergency room, Williamson kept asking the nurses for updates on the TCU game. The nurses repeatedly asked him if he wanted to see a chaplain. He said, no, but a doctor would be nice. "He's a very committed Christian," Patty said about her husband's not wanting to see a minister. "His heart is fine with the Lord."

After a 90-minute procedure, Williamson was in the intensive-care unit lamenting the absence of a television. That's when Patty told her son that since San Diego State had rallied and gotten close they wouldn't talk about the game until it was over.

After the game, the offensive line turned a planned cookout into an impromptu prayer session for their coach. "It was like I was with my brothers, and we were praying for our dad," said tackle Marcus Cannon.

Williamson was back on the sideline for the Rose Bowl. "The one thing I found out through all of this is I love life," he said. "I want to stay alive, but I'm not afraid to die, either."

Some fears are universal; others are particular. Speaking to the Rotary Club may require a heavy dose of antiperspirant. Elevator walls may feel as though they're closing in on you. And don't even get started on being in the dark with spiders and snakes during a thunderstorm.

We all live in fear, and God knows this. Dozens of passages in the Bible urge us not to be afraid. God isn't telling us to lose our wariness of oncoming cars or big dogs with nasty dispositions; these are helpful fears God instilled in us for our own protection. What God does wish driven from our lives is a spirit of fear that dominates us, that makes our lives miserable and keeps us from doing what we should, such as sharing our faith.

In commanding that we not be afraid, God reminds us that when we trust him completely, we find peace that calms our fears.

I am a person of faith. I'm not afraid to die, but I didn't want to.
— Eddie Williamson after his heart attack

You have your own peculiar set of fears,
but they should never paralyze you
because God is greater than anything you fear.

KEEPING THE PEACE

Read Hebrews 12:14-17.

"Make every effort to live in peace with all men and to be holy" (v. 14).

An enraged TCU football player once started an all-out riot by throwing a punch -- at an official.

At 6-3, the Frogs were solid underdogs against undefeated Rice on Nov. 24, 1934, in Houston. They used one magnificent drive and some stalwart defense, however, to pull off a 7-2 upset.

TCU actually won the game on its first possession. Led by junior halfback Jimmy Lawrence, who was All-Southwest Conference in both 1933 and '35, the Frogs marched 80 yards for a score. Behind solid blocking from Taldon Manton and George Kline, Lawrence rushed for most of the yardage on the drive. Then from the Owl 6, he passed to team captain Joe Coleman for the game's lone TD.

The score came on a busted play. Lawrence had apparently been dropped for a 10-yard loss when he spotted Coleman nearby. He broke a tackle and tossed the ball in desperation. Coleman made the catch at the 13 and took it in. Manton booted the PAT.

After that, Walter Roach, a three-time all-conference tight end, and Darrell Lester, a two-time All-American center, led a defense that kept the powerful Owls out of the end zone. Rice's only score came in the fourth quarter when the Frogs intentionally gave up a safety to avoid punting from the end zone against a stiff wind.

But then came the most serious Rice threat of the game. After the punt, the field judge called interference on a Rice pass, thus setting the Owls in business at the TCU 9. The Frog defense held, though, with Rice's last try ending at the 4.

When the game ended, Lawrence, apparently still upset at what was generally viewed as a bad pass interference call, ran onto the field and knocked the offending official out with one solid punch to the jaw. That kicked off a riot that lasted about 15 minutes and ended only when a squad of policemen showed up.

Perhaps you've never been in a brawl or a public brouhaha to match the one Jimmy Lawrence started with one punch. But maybe you retaliated when you got one elbow too many in a pickup basketball game. Or maybe you and your spouse or your teenager get into it occasionally, shouting and saying cruel things. Or road rage may be a part of your life.

While we do seem to live in a more belligerent, confrontational society than ever before, fighting is still not the solution to a problem. Rather, it only escalates the whole confrontation, leaving wounded pride, intransigence, and simmering hatred in its wake. Actively seeking and making peace is the way to a solution that lasts and heals broken relationships and aching hearts.

Peacemaking is not as easy as fighting, but it is much more courageous and a lot less painful. It is also exactly what Jesus would do.

There was a great deal of excitement and some pushing and punching but no one was hurt and police finally cleared the gridiron.
-- Writer Flem Hall on the 1934 Rice brawl

Making peace instead of fighting takes courage
and strength; it's also what Jesus would do.

ROCK SOLID

Read Luke 6:46-49.

"I will show you what he is like who comes to me and hears my words and puts them into practice. He is like a man building a house, who dug down deep and laid the foundation on rock" (vv. 47-48).

Janice Dziuk wasn't around for the many seasons of 20+ wins the TCU women have racked up, but she helped lay the foundation for them all.

On the occasion of Dziuk's induction into the TCU Hall of Fame in 2002, the first women's basketball player to receive the honor, a writer said she was "a memorable player who didn't play on the most memorable teams." In fact, Dziuk wanted it that way.

Coming out of high school in 1986, she had her pick of schools. She chose TCU, which had no women's basketball tradition at the time. "I wanted to go where I could play," she said, and "do something that could make a difference or build a foundation for someone else down the road."

At TCU, she did just that. From 1986-1990, Dziuk was the program's first star. She was First-Team All-Southwest Conference and the TCU Athlete of the Year her senior season. She was named to the Southwest Conference All-Decade Team of the 1980s. An award named after her is presented each year to the TCU player who exemplifies work ethic, attitude, and team concept.

Decades later, Dziuk's name is still all over the school's record book: second in scoring average and free throws made; third in field goals made, rebounds, and points scored; and eighth in steals and field goal percentage.

The wins weren't plentiful; her four teams won a combined 40 games. What Dziuk accomplished, however laid the foundation for the program's later success that included nine trips to the NCAA Tournament in eleven seasons and ten seasons of at least 20 wins in eleven years.

Like TCU's athletics program, your life is an ongoing project, a work in progress. As with any successful sports program, if your life is to be stable, it must have a solid foundation, which holds everything up and keeps everything together.

R. Alan Culpepper said in *The New Interpreter's Bible*, "We do not choose whether we will face severe storms in life; we only get to choose the foundation on which we will stand." In other words, tough times are inevitable. If your foundation isn't rock solid, you will have nothing on which to stand as those storms buffet you, nothing to keep your life from flying apart into a cycle of disappointment and destruction.

But when the foundation is solid and sure, you can take the blows, stand strong, recover, and live with joy and hope. Only one foundation is sure and foolproof: Jesus Christ. Everything else you build upon will fail you.

She really did lay a foundation for our basketball players to follow.
-- TCU women's basketball coach Jeff Mittie on Janice Dziuk

In the building of your life, you must start with a foundation in Jesus Christ, or the first trouble that shows up will knock you down.

CONFIDENCE MAN

Read Micah 7:5-7.

"As for me, I will look to the Lord, I will wait for the God of my salvation" (v. 7 NRSV).

The Horned Frogs walked right into the collegiate equivalent of the Valley of Death, but they were so confident that they were not the least bit intimidated.

As strange as it may sound, TCU's 2009 football season hinged on the third game, and it wasn't even a conference battle. "This game is going to tell a lot," declared running back Joseph Turner. "There's no way we can reach all our goals and lose this game."

It wasn't even a game the Frogs were originally scheduled to play. TCU was to meet Houston for its third game, but conflicts from the Cougar side canceled it. An ACC program also needed a game that weekend, and the AD offered TCU $1 million to come play. The Frogs took the deal. As head coach Gary Patterson put it, "With the budget and payday we were going to get, it was a win."

Who was this "pedigreed opponent" with its legendary and fearsome home field advantage? The Clemson Tigers. On Sept. 26, the Frogs strode into a place so loud and so intimidating that its well-deserved nickname is Death Valley. The screams of about 70,000 berserk, orange-clad Clemson fans several times forced TCU quarterback Andy Dalton to use a silent snap count.

The Frogs played like they feared nothing, refusing to let "the day's growing drama get the better of them." They kept their poise, moving the ball "with confidence on offense behind an experienced quarterback [Dalton], who probably played his best game." On defense, the Frogs "stood tall among the heavy raindrops."

Early in the fourth quarter, Dalton lofted a pass that sophomore wide receiver Antoine Hicks claimed for a 25-yard touchdown. It was "the kind of aggressive play that a confident, battle-tested offense makes on the road." The score was the difference in the 14-10 win that propelled the Frogs to a 12-0 season capped off by the program's first-ever BCS bowl.

You need confidence in all areas of your life. You're confident the company you work for will pay you on time, or you wouldn't go to work. You turn the ignition confident your car will start. When you flip a switch, you expect the light to come on.

Confidence in other people and in things is often misplaced, though. Companies go broke; car batteries die; light bulbs burn out. Even the people you love the most sometimes let you down.

So where can you place your trust with absolute confidence you won't be betrayed? In the promises of God.

Such confidence is easy when everything's going your way, but what about when you cry as Micah did, "What misery is mine!" As Micah declares, that's when your confidence in God must be its strongest. That's when you wait for the Lord confident that God will not fail you, that he will never let you down.

We gained a lot of confidence as a football team.
-- Gary Patterson on the win over Clemson

**People, things, and organizations will let you
down; only God can be trusted
with absolute and unfailing confidence.**

HEAD GAMES

Read Philippians 4:4-9.

"Do not be anxious about anything, . . . And the God of peace will be with you" (vv. 6a, 9b).

Sarah Scherer had to shoot in the Olympics when every shot meant pain.

Finishing up at TCU in 2013, Scherer was only the tenth participant in NCAA rifle shooting to earn All-America honors in both air rifle and smallbore all four years. She was also a two-time smallbore national champion. She shot for two national champions at TCU, the 2010 team becoming the first-ever all-female rifle team to win the NCAA title in the coed sport.

In a sport that requires mental toughness like no other, Scherer had to battle through painful distractions that redefined the limits of her concentration and focus. In October of 2010, when Scherer was a sophomore, her brother committed suicide. He had introduced her to competitive shooting and had participated in the 2008 Olympics. She had been there, cheering him on.

When she made the U.S. Olympic team in 2012 and arrived in London, the memories closed in on her. She said her brother "is always with me. He's a part of who I am." Her return to the Olympics, therefore, in itself required mental toughness.

But Scherer was also battling physical pain that threatened to destroy her focus. Only five days before she was to leave with the U.S. team and only two weeks before she was to shoot, Scherer slipped on a wet floor at a friend's house. The fall dislocated her left elbow and fractured the radial head. "It was one of those pains where you wish you could faint from it," she said.

While everybody else was making last-minute preparations for the Olympics, Scherer couldn't take a practice shot for two weeks. Even then, the elbow hurt when she shot.

Thus, on July 28, in the Olympics, every shot sent pain shooting through her elbow. She knew it was coming, but she was still mentally tough enough to finish seventh.

As Sarah Scherer's young life illustrates, persevering in American society today generally necessitates mental strength. Your job, your family, your finances, just getting everything done every day -- they all demand mental toughness from you by placing stress upon you to perform. Stress is a fact of life, though it isn't all bad as you are often led to believe. Stress can lead you to function at your best. Rather than buckling under it, you stand up, make constant decisions, and keep going.

So it is with your faith life. "Too blessed to be stressed" sounds nice, but followers of Jesus Christ know all about stress. Society screams compromise; your children whine about being cool; your company ignores ethics. But you don't fold beneath the stress; you keep your mind on Christ and the way he said to live because you are tough mentally, strengthened by your faith. After all, you have God's word and God's grace for relief and support.

Sarah is tough. She has self-control. She's a tough young lady.
                                            -- Sarah Scherer's mother

**Toughened mentally by your faith in Christ,
you live out what you believe, and you persevere.**

AD MAN

Read Mark 1:21-28.

"News about him spread quickly over the whole region"
(v. 28).

As the 2010 season progressed and the Frogs kept winning, head coach Gary Patterson turned into the program's number-one advertising and public relations man.

TCU was 11-0 and ranked third in the nation on Nov. 19 when Patterson spent the day at ESPN headquarters in Bristol, Conn., "and effectively turned it into a series of soapbox opportunities." The head Frog's message was pretty much one-dimensional but important: His team belonged with the big boys.

The ESPN bigwigs must have believed it because they pretty much turned their studios over to Patterson, giving him what they call the "car wash" treatment. He began the whirlwind day with a visit to *Mike & Mike in the Morning*, sitting behind the pair's usual assortment of bobbleheads.

Then it was on to *First Take* with Mike Hill. By 11:30, Patterson was in the cafeteria grabbing a quick lunch. Media relations director Mark Cohen was there also, declaring on his cell phone, "They love us, it seems. It's fantastic exposure."

The exposure continued with seven minutes on Scott Van Pelt's radio show. "I'm here today . . . to let people know what kind of people and what kind of football team we have at TCU," Patterson said. Then it was on to *SportsCenter*, ESPN's crown jewel, before

HORNED FROGS

a 12-minute segment on *College Football Live* with the head coach rared back in an overstuffed chair.

Patterson's whirlwind media blitz wasn't over, though. After his last appearance in Bristol ended at 3 p.m., he hopped a jet to Chicago. Saturday morning, he appeared live on the set of *College GameDay* from Wrigley Field.

Gary Patterson got the word out about his Frogs.

Commercials and advertisements for products, goods, and services inundate us. Watch NASCAR: Decals cover the cars and the drivers' uniforms. Turn on your computer and ads pop up. TV, radio, newspapers, billboards, every square inch of every wall -- everyone's one trying to get the word out the best way possible.

Jesus was no different in that he used the most effective and efficient means of advertising he had at his disposal to spread his message of salvation and hope among the masses. That was word of mouth.

In his ministry, Jesus didn't isolate himself; instead, he moved from town to town among the common folks, preaching, teaching, and healing. Those who encountered Jesus then told others about their experience, thus spreading the news about the good news.

Almost two millennia later, nothing's really changed. Speaking to someone else about Jesus remains the best way to get the word out, and the best advertisement of all is a changed life.

I'm here [because] I owe it to my team to let the world know that [they] are worthy of playing on the biggest stage in college football.
-- Gary Patterson during his ESPN blitz

The best advertising for Jesus is word of mouth, telling others what he has done for you.

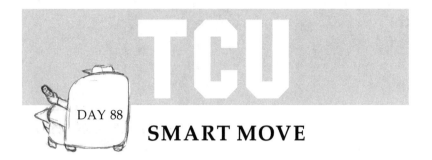

SMART MOVE

Read 1 Kings 4:29-34; 11:1-6.

"[Solomon] was wiser than any other man. . . . As Solomon grew old, his wives turned his heart after other gods, and his heart was not fully devoted to the Lord his God" (vv. 4:31, 11:4).

His team in trouble, head coach Abe Martin made a smart move: He asked his players for some ideas.

Led by All-American defensive tackle Bob Lilly, the Horned Frogs of 1959 were a talented bunch. Described as "college football's greatest defensive tackle," Lilly started for TCU as a sophomore, was All-Southwest Conference as a junior in 1959, and was All-America as a senior. He was the first player ever drafted by the Dallas Cowboys and is a member of the NFL and the college football halls of fame. Also on that 1959 team was Don Floyd, an All-American tackle in both 1958 and '59. End Buddy Iles was a sophomore who would go on to twice earn first-team All-SWC honors. Jack Spikes was an All-American running back.

And yet with all that talent, "we were sputtering offensively," said starting end Paul Peebles. Worse than that, the team was losing. After beating Kansas 14-7 in the opener, the Frogs lost two in a row, both shutouts.

So Martin called a team meeting to discuss what was going on. Rather than berate his players, the head coach asked them for suggestions. Starting center Avre Martin recalled that the seniors had one: start fellow senior Jackie Sledge at quarterback. The head coach then made another smart move; he took their advice.

Behind Sledge, the Frogs rolled through the rest of the season unbeaten, seven straight wins, and landed in Houston in the first-ever Bluebonnet Bowl. "There was a special feeling with that man at quarterback," Peebles said. "We felt no one could stop us."

We don't always make moves as smart as the ones Abe Martin made in 1959. Remember that time you wrecked the car when you spilled hot coffee on your lap? That cold morning you fell out of the boat? Don't even talk about locking your keys in the car.

Formal education notwithstanding, we all make some dumb moves sometimes because time spent in a classroom is not an accurate gauge of common sense. Folks impressed with their own smarts often grace us with erudite pronouncements that we intuitively recognize as flawed, unworkable, or simply wrong.

A good example is the observation that great intelligence and scholarship are inherently incompatible with a deep and abiding faith in God. That is, the more we know, the less we believe. Any incompatibility occurs, however, only because we begin to trust in our own wisdom rather than the wisdom of God. We forget, as Solomon did, that God is the ultimate source of all our knowledge and wisdom and that even our ability to learn is a gift from God.

Not smart at all.

If we'd gone with Jackie Sledge from the beginning, we could've really been something.
                                                    -- Paul Peebles on the 1959 team

**Being truly smart means trusting in God's
wisdom rather than only in our own knowledge.**

TOUGH COOKIES

Read 2 Corinthians 11:21b-29.

"Besides everything else, I face daily the pressure of my concern for all the churches" (v. 28).

If the TCU defense could play tough, the Frogs might give Texas a game. As it turned out, the defense was plenty tough enough.

TCU had not beaten Texas at home since 1958 when the 20th-ranked Longhorns came to town on Nov. 7, 1992. The chances of ending that horrendous streak didn't look too good -- especially on the defensive side of the ball.

The truth is that TCU was outmanned. "We've got mostly 210-to 220-pound linemen, and we have one linebacker who's 185 pounds," said TCU defensive coordinator Reggie Herring. "We're going against their 300-pounders on the offensive line. People have no idea just how tough it is." Texas did have some rather big chunks of beef on its side of the ball, fielding an offensive line that averaged 280 pounds. Behind that mass of humanity, the Horns went into the game averaging 428 yards of offense per game.

But that wasn't all working against the defense; it was flat-out banged up. End Tunji Bolden fought off a hip flexor to get in for a few plays. Brad Wallace, his counterpart on the other side of the line, suffered a leg injury during the game and managed to get back onto the field down the stretch. Tackle Brian Brooks toughed it out and played despite a stress fracture in his leg. Then there was linebacker Brad Smith, injured so badly that he limped after

HORNED FROGS

every play. He played on "despite a list of injuries that would send most players to the sideline."

So that outmanned and banged-up defense "went out and showed guts and character," Herring said after the game. They held the Horns to 228 total yards and only 52 yards rushing. Behind that tough defense, the Frogs pulled off the upset 23-14.

"The key to this victory was heart," asserted TCU head coach Pat Sullivan. That and a whole lot of toughness on defense.

You don't have to be a TCU defender to be tough. In America today, toughness isn't restricted to physical accomplishments and brute strength. Going to work every morning even when you feel bad, sticking by your rules for your children in a society that ridicules parental authority, making hard decisions about your aging parents' care often over their objections — you've got to be tough every day just to live honorably, decently, and justly.

Living faithfully requires toughness, too, though in America chances are you won't be imprisoned, stoned, or flogged this week for your faith as Paul was. Still, contemporary society exerts subtle, psychological, daily pressures on you to turn your back on your faith and your values. Popular culture promotes promiscuity, atheism, and gutter language; your children's schools have kicked God out; the corporate culture advocates amorality before the shrine of the almighty dollar.

You have to hang tough to keep the faith.

Our coaches convinced us we could win if we play 'guts out' football.
— Linebacker Brad Smith on the '92 win over Texas

Life demands more than mere physical toughness; you must be spiritually tough too.

CASE OF THE NERVES

Read Mark 5:1-20.

"What do you want with me, Jesus, Son of the Most High God? Swear to God that you won't torture me!" (v. 7)

TCU's "unbeatable assassin" was nervous, and his first pitches showed it.

One writer said of Matt Purke that he "looks like a goofball on the mound, with his sideways-turned cap and black-rimmed prescription glasses." But, that same writer said, despite that appearance, the TCU freshman was "an unbeatable assassin."

That was in 2010 when Purke, the best pitcher in college baseball, led the Horned Frogs to their first-ever appearance in the College World Series. He had been drafted in the first round in 2009 by the Texas Rangers, but the negotiations fell through.

Purke set a school record and led the nation with sixteen wins. He didn't lose a single game, striking out 142 batters in 116 innings. He won practically every award a freshman could, including the National Freshman of the Year.

But Purke was still only a year removed from high school and hadn't pitched on any stage to equal that on which he stood on June 19. He was the starting pitcher for TCU's first-ever game in the College World Series. And he was nervous.

The first FSU batter slapped a leadoff single. Then an infield error on a chopper left Purke behind 1-0 with a runner on third. That's when All-American catcher Bryan Holaday trotted to the mound for a conference. "Hey, this is all on you," he told Purke. "Just regroup. . . . Pitch like there's not a runner on third, and do your thing." In other words, settle down and do what you've done all season.

Purke did. He struck out the next three batters, and when the offense scored five times in the bottom of the first, the game was essentially over. FSU had missed its chance to take advantage of Purke's nervous start. TCU won easily 8-1.

Unlike Matt Purke in Omaha, we often can't really explain why some situations make us nervous. Making a speech, for instance. Or being in the presence of a person we'd like to ask out.

We probably rarely if ever consider the possibility that we make other people nervous. Who in the world could be intimidated by us? Try this on for starters: Satan himself. Yep, that very demon of darkness that Hollywood repeatedly portrays as so powerful that goodness is helpless before him. That's the one.

But we can make Satan nervous only if we stand before him with the power of Jesus Christ at our disposal. As Christians, we seem to understand that our basic mission is to further Jesus' kingdom and change the world through emulating him in the way we live and love others. But do we appreciate that in truly living for Jesus, we are daily tormenting the very devil himself?

Satan and his lackeys quake helplessly in fear and nervousness before the power of almighty God that is in us through Jesus.

The more that he's cornered, the better that he is.
-- TCU head coach Jim Schlossnagle on Matt Purke's shaky start

Nervous and apprehensive -- so stands Satan
himself in the presence of a follower of Jesus.

THE PRIZE

Read Philippians 3:10-16.

"I press on toward the goal to win the prize for which God has called me heavenward in Christ Jesus" (v. 14).

One of college football's more unusual trophies is a piece of cookware.

With only a handful of miles separating their two campuses, a rivalry between TCU and SMU was born early in college football history. They first played in 1915, a 43-0 TCU win.

The rivalry was fierce after World War II when college football boomed as athletes who had been soldiers came home and took advantage of the GI Bill. Prior to the 1946 game, SMU's Student Council proposed that a trophy be awarded to the winner. TCU's council liked the idea, so the two groups met in Dallas to hash out the rules for a traveling trophy. Thus was born the Iron Skillet.

SMU won the game, and the two student councils met at a Dallas restaurant to present the inaugural trophy. Derrell Tipps, TCU's student body president, quipped, "It was their idea, so we had to let them win the first one."

Over the years, though, interest in the trophy waned, and the original skillet was lost. In 1993, both schools agreed to resurrect the tradition, and "a new Iron Skillet was brought to the table." This one was cast iron and weighed about thirty pounds. Today, the trophy is presented to the winning team's athletic department rather than to the student council.

HORNED FROGS

One of the mysteries surrounding the strange trophy is why it's a skillet. An old story asserts that in the 1950s an SMU fan was frying frog legs before a game as something of a joke. An affronted TCU fan said that eating frog legs went too far and suggested that they should let the game decide who got the skillet and the food. TCU won, and the skillet and the legs were handed over.

While that story may be fun, it's certainly not true since it conflicts with the officially published report of the student councils' meeting to establish the award.

Even the most modest and self-effacing among us can't help but be pleased by prizes and honors. They symbolize the approval and appreciation of others, whether it's a strange sports trophy, an Employee of the Month trophy, a plaque for sales achievement, or the sign declaring yours as the neighborhood's prettiest yard.

Such prizes and awards are often the culmination of the pursuit of personal achievement and accomplishment. They represent accolades and recognition from the world. Nothing is inherently wrong with any of that as long as we keep them in perspective.

That is, we must never let awards become such idols that we worship or lower our sight from the greatest prize of all and the only one truly worth winning. It's one that won't rust, collect dust, or leave us wondering why we worked so hard to win it in the first place. The ultimate prize is eternal life, and it's ours through Jesus Christ.

The Battle for the Iron Skillet. SMU vs. TCU. A Tradition since 1915.
-- Inscription on the Iron Skillet

**God has the greatest prize of all ready
to hand to you through Jesus Christ.**

FOOD FOR THOUGHT

Read Genesis 9:1-7.

"Everything that lives and moves will be food for you. Just as I gave you the green plants, I now give you everything" (v. 3).

Robert Deck had to learn quickly all the nuances of a brand new position. He also had a special directive: eat, eat, and eat.

Deck walked on at TCU as a tight end in 2007 and earned a scholarship. He was redshirted, saw limited action for the next two seasons, and then played in twelve games as a junior in 2010. As Deck's senior season approached, he looked forward to catching his first-ever pass.

Two weeks before August camp began, though, his final year took an unexpected turn when he was asked to move to offensive tackle to provide some depth. "I never saw it coming," Deck said. "I never thought I'd go back to putting my hand in the dirt every play." Realizing the move would put him on the field more, Deck readily agreed.

What followed was a crash course at which Deck was so adept that he made a "mockery out of other linemen's years of studying and working in the trenches honing their craft." Deck was so good so quickly that when the season began, he was the starting right tackle. "He has been playing out of his mind," said Jeff Olson, who moved to left tackle to accommodate Deck.

Deck was also very good at a less demanding aspect of his position change; his coaches told him he had to eat -- and eat some more. His fellow offensive linemen, especially left guard Spencer Thompson, ensured that Deck ate like one of them. "He's cooking all the time and I"m right there next to him trying everything he pulls out of the oven," Deck said.

Deck ate quite well, moving from 260 to 290 pounds.

Belly up to the buffet, boys and girls, for barbecue, sirloin steak, grilled chicken, and fried catfish with hush puppies and cheese grits. Rachael Ray's a household name; hamburger joints, pizza parlors, and taco stands lurk on every corner; and we have a TV channel devoted exclusively to food. We love our chow.

Food is one of God's really good ideas, but consider the complex divine plan that begins with a kernel and winds up with corn-on-the-cob slathered with butter and littered with salt. The creator of all life devised a downright fascinating and effective system in which living things are sustained and nourished physically through the sacrifice of other living things in a way similar to what Christ underwent to save us spiritually.

Whether it's fast food or home-cooked, practically everything we eat is a gift from God secured through a divine plan in which some plants and/or animals have given up their lives. Pausing to give thanks before we dive in seems the least we can do.

The other day we had a gathering for the Rangers game and we killed three pork roasts.
-- Robert Deck on eating like an offensive lineman

God created a system that nourishes us through the sacrifice of other living things; that's worth a thank-you.

NOTES
(by Devotion Day Number)

1   "our boys fought the game . . . the Houston Heavyweights team.": "First Game, First Victory," *Greatest Moments in TCU Football History,* Dan Jenkins and Francis J. Fitzgerald, eds. (Louisville, Kent.: AdCraft Sports Marketing, 1996), p. 27.

1   The AddRan boys were too strong for Toby's team.: "First Game, First Victory," *Greatest Moments in TCU Football History,* p. 27.

2   the worst game of his career.: Brian Bennett, "'Locked In' Andy Dalton Finds Redemption," *ESPN. com,* Jan. 1, 2011, http://espn.go.com/blog/NCFNation/post/_/id/36923/locked-in.

2   Dalton took much of the blame . . . didn't want to feel again,": Bennett, "'Locked-In' Andy Dalton."

2   He quit cracking jokes . . . everything they were doing.": Bennett, "'Locked-In' Andy Dalton."

2   "the guy who led this team . . . job to finish it off,": Bennett, "'Locked-In' Andy Dalton."

2   I was really focused . . . to play well in this game.: Bennett, "'Locked-In' Andy Dalton."

3   the greatest at-bat in TCU . . . of the College World Series.: "Instant Classic -- 'Rally Turtle Sends Frogs into Frenzy,'" *CollegeBaseball360.com,* June 24, 2010, http://collegebaseball360. com/2010/06/24/rally-turtle-sends-frogs-into-frenzy.

3   "immediately turned to the . . . home run of his life.": "Instant Classic," *CollegeBaseball360.com.*

3   When Curry turned to . . . prepared to make a catch.: "Instant Classic," *CollegeBaseball360.com.*

3   "Schlossnagle said he wanted . . . the ball in the lights.: Brian Bennett, "Frogs Drawn to a Rally," *ESPN.com,* June 23, 2010, http://sports.espn.go.com/ncaa/news/story?id=5321590.

3   "one of the greatest moments in the history of [the college world series].": "Instant Classic," *CollegeBaseball360.com.*

3   Perhaps the greatest comeback in the TCU program's history.: "Instant Classic," *CollegeBaseball 360.com.*

4   "I'd rather be tall than a squatty body,": John Underwood, "A Big Ol' Country Boy," *Sports Illustrated,* Oct. 15, 1962, http://sportsillustrated.cnn.com/vault/article/magazine/MAG1074203/ index.htm.

4   after his studies began. . . visits home to Graham.: Underwood, "A Big Ol' Country Boy."

4   Pepper was described, somewhat vaguely, . . . "Pepper really scared 'em,": Underwood, "A Big Ol' Country Boy."

4   She wouldn't hurt anyone. . . . on you a little bit.: Underwood, "A Big Ol' Country Boy."

5   safety Byron Linwood stopped the Hog back at the TCU 12,: Mike Jones, "TCU Stuns Arkansas, 32-31," *Greatest Moments in TCU Football History,* p. 186.

5   When he got to the . . . the play he had called.: Jones, "TCU Stuns Arkansas, 32-31," *Greatest Moments in TCU Football History,* p. 187.

5   The play was designed to go to Davis in the flat, but he was covered.: Jones, "TCU Stuns Arkansas, 32-31," *Greatest Moments in TCU Football History,* p. 187.

5   I saw that [Anthony] Gulley . . . they're gonna get him.': Jones, "TCU Stuns Arkansas, 32-31," *Greatest Moments in TCU Football History,* p. 187.

6   The Frogs would stop Peterson . . . in his first career start.: "TKO'd by TCU, " *SI.com,* Sept. 3, 2005, http://sportsillustrated.cnn.com/vault/article/web/COM1038880/index/index.htm.

6   A man without a plan doesn't have a future.: Joe Drape, "Assembling More Than a Football Program at T.C.U.," *The New York Times,* Aug 27, 2011, http://www.nytimes.com/2011/08/28/ sports/ncaafootball0/at-tcu-the-football-coach-gary-patterson.

7   She once said that she . . . I was really seeing it,": Rick Waters, "Success Comes in Threes," *The TCU Magazine,* Winter 2006, http://www.magarchive.tcu.edu/articles/2006-01-rr4.asp.

7   The first time Mittie . . . and to get stronger.: Waters, "Success Comes in Threes."

7   If you coach for 25 . . . that is success.: Susie Magill, "Coales of Wisdom," *Sharing the Victory,* March 2009, http://sharingthevictory.com/vsItemDisplay.1sp?.

8   "kinda shuffling around and mumbling . . . out there all fired up.": Whit Canning, "Berry Outduels Walker in Final Meeting," *Greatest Moments in TCU Football History,* p. 111.

8   In the locker room after . . . two days before the SMU game.: Canning, "Berry Outduels Walker in Final Meeting," *Greatest Moments in TCU Football History,* p. 111.

8   He never actually gave a straight answer.: Canning, "Berry Outduels Walker in Final Meeting," *Greatest Moments in TCU Football History,* p. 111.

9   the program's "all-time greatest upset": Stefan Stevenson, "TCU's Upset of Kansas Feels Like a Distant Memory," *Star-Telegram.com,* Feb. 22, 2013, http://nl.newsbank.com/nl-search/we/ Archives/p_action=doc&p_docid=1449F7192BDF8.

9   "one of the most improbable upsets in recent college basketball history.": Stefan Stevenson, "Frog

Heaven: TCU Rocks Kansas," *Star-Telegram.com*, Feb. 7, 2013, http://nl.newsbank.com/nl-search/we/Archives?p_action=doc&p_docid=1444DB6092A3A.

9   TCU never trailed; the Frogs scored . . . seven minutes into the game.: Stevenson, "Frog Heaven: TCU Rocks Kansas."

9   With 6:19 to go in the first half, KU had two points.: Mac Engel, "TCU's KO of KU, Though Not Pretty, Is Something to Admire," *Star-Telegram.com*, Feb. 7, 2013, http://nl.newsbank.com/nl-search/we/Archives?p_action=doc&p_docid=1444DB5FF7D55.

9   "TCU believed it could win, and was out-playing" Kansas.": Engel, "TCU's KO of KU."

9   Jerry Palm of *CBSSports.com* . . . I've been tracking numbers.": Stefan Stevenson, "Wake-Up Call," *Star-Telegram.com*, Feb. 8, 2013. http://nl.newsbank.com/nl-search/we/Archives?p_action=doc&p_docid-14452FA9E64516.

9   A frenetic, I-don't-believe-what-I-just-saw moment.: Stevenson, "TCU's Upset of Kansas."

10   the first time the whole season the Frogs had been behind.: Flem Hall, "No. 1 TCU Tops Carnegie Tech," *Greatest Moments in TCU Football History*, p. 73.

10   The Frogs got off the floor to win.: Hall, "No. 1 TCU Tops Carnegie Tech," *Greatest Moments in TCU Football History*, p. 73.

11   Most of the experts pegged TCU as a two-to-three touchdown underdog,: Flem Hall, "Horned Frogs Shock Ohio State, 18-14," *Greatest Moments in TCU Football History*, p. 146.

11   who had moved into the starting lineup during the week,: Hall, "Horned Frogs Shock Ohio State,, 18-14," *Greatest Moments in TCU Football History*, p. 146.

11   The starters were obviously . . . sent in the entire second team.: Hall, "Horned Frogs Shock Ohio State, 18-14," *Greatest Moments in TCU Football History*, p. 146.

12   "He was the only person . . . and I was ready.": "Freshman Jackson Leads TCU to 17-7 Comeback Victory over Baylor," *GoFrogs.cstv.com*, Sept. 3, 2006, http://gofrogs.cstv.com/m-footbl/recaps/090306aaa.html.

12   It was crazy. . . . maybe three or four.": "Freshman Jackson Leads TCU to 17-7 Comeback."

13   Corley was a basketball and . . . to earn her way back.": Rick Waters, "At Home on the Court," *The TCU Magazine*, Fall 2007, http://www.magarchive.tcu.edu/articles/2007-04-RR6.asp.

13   I think I needed to . . . couldn't live without volleyball.: Waters, "At Home on the Court."

14   "I knew I wasn't going . . . decided not to go,": Beau Tiongson, "Former Frog Finds Spot on Depth Chart in Italy," *tcu360.com*, April 29, 2013, http://www.tcu360.com/football/2013/04/18013.

14   he received an email . . . where the Lord put him.: Tiongson, "Former Frog Lands Spot."

14   "a touchdown has the same meaning in any language.": Tiongson, "Former Frog Lands Spot."

15   TCU marched through "realignment wilderness": Andy Staples, "TCU's March Through Realignment Wilderness Finally Comes to an End," *SI.com*, July 5, 2012, http://sportsillustrated.cnn.com/2012/writers/andy_staples/07/05/tcu-big-12-realignment.

15   "People at TCU still stew . . . conference landscape of college athletics: Staples, "TCU's March."

15   TCU has traveled a long . . . like to welcome you home.: Staples, "TCU's March."

16   The Frogs' coaching staff knew . . . its dominant offensive line.: "TCU Denies Wisconsin on Late 2-Point Try to Win Rose Bowl," *ESPN.com*, Jan. 1, 2011. http://scores.espn.go.com/ncf/recap?gameId=310012628.

16   the Badgers lined up in . . . and a safety racing in.: Brian Bennett, "Tank Carder in Right Place, Time for TCU," *ESPN.com*, Jan. 1, 2011, http://espn.go.com/blog/NFCNations/post_/id36943.

16   A mistake in the Frogs' . . . open in the end zone.: Bennett, "Tank Carder in Right Place."

16   "I went to go blitz . . . get through the hole,": Stefan Stevenson, "TCU Finishes with Perfect Season, with Rose Bowl Win," *Believe It* (Chicago,: Triumph Books, 2011), p. 10.

16   the Horned Frogs are lucky Carder is so good.": Bennett, "Tank Carder in Right Place."

16   We were lucky Tank was in the game.": Bennett, "Tank Carder in Right Place."

17   "I think today showed . . . we have to play like it.": Stefan Stevenson, "TCU Crushes Flyers to Stay Alive," *Star-Telegram. com*, June 3, 2012, http://nl.newsbank.com/nl-search/we/Archives?p_action+doc&p_docid=13F695EE9B338.

17   "despicable, vile, unprincipled scoundrels.": John MacArthur, *Twelve Ordinary Men* (Nashville: W Publishing Group, 2002), p. 152.

17   You get your back . . . about people a little bit.: Stevenson, "TCU Crushes Flyers to Stay Alive."

18   He was so overcome . . . I've ever witnessed.": Whit Canning, "TCU Upsets Sixth-ranked Texas A&M," *Greatest Moments in TCU Football History*, p. 112.

19   "Going into the game, . . . was winning the game.": "Running to a Record," *cnnsi.com*, Nov. 21, 1999, http://sportsillustrated.cnn.com/football/college/news/1999/11/20/tomlinson_record.

19   If he's close to . . . let him finish it off.: "Running to a Record."

20   Lee Corso -- who had predicted that Oregon State would beat TCU by three touchdowns: Stefan Stevenson, "Thank You, Lee Corso," *Believe It!*, p. 36.

TCU

20   He had barely stepped out . . . with tape of the Bears.: Stefan Stevenson, "As Expected, the No. 4-Ranked Horned Frogs Had Little Trouble," *Believe It!*, p. 42.

20   "We have to be ready . . . like the fourth-ranked team in the nation." Stevenson, "As Expected, the No. 4-Ranked Horned Frogs Had Little Trouble," *Believe It!*, p. 46.

20   I wasn't surprised.: Stefan Stevenson, "A 35-3 Halftime Lead Shows How Big the Gap Is," *Believe It!*, p. 54.

21   The house where she lived . . . she took the advice.: Rick Waters, "Redemption in the Crosshairs." *The TCU Magazine*, spring 2006, http://www.magarchive.tcu.edu/articles/2006-02-RR6.asp.

21   Basically, [Monez] took me . . . built me back up.: Waters, "Redemption in the Crosshairs."

22   Studying films in preparation . . . left hand up for the block: Stefan Stevenson, "Assist on Verrett's Block Goes to Coach," *Star-Telegram.com*, Nov. 4, 2012, http://nl.newsbank.com/nl-search/we/Archives?p_action=doc&p_docid=1426B47BB6A80.

22   Coach Bump called me . . . a big play right here.': Stevenson, "Assist on Verrett's Block."

23   He donned full pads . . . had 13 tackles.: John Waters, "College Football," *Sports Illustrated*, Sept. 26, 1994, http://sportsillustrated.cnn.com/vault/article/magazine/MAG1005729/index.htm.

23   I haven't always started, but I certainly never quit,": Waters, "College Football."

23   I needed a scholarship, ... I have my dreams.: Waters, "College Football."

24   "We did have some mistakes," . . . to take care of.": Stefan Stevenson, "As Expected, the No. 4-Ranked Horned Frogs Had Little Trouble," *Believe It*, p. 44.

24   Fifth-year senior Ryan . . . "I'm happy for him.": Stevenson, "As Expected," *Believe It!*, p. 42.

24   I want to publicly . . . to score the last touchdown.: Stevenson, "As Expected," *Believe It!*, p. 42.

25   a coach "who builds college basketball programs.": "End of an Era," *The TCU Magazine*, Winter 2001, http://www.magarchive.tcu.edu/articles/2001-04-RR.asp2.

25   he promised Billyball, saying . . . every minute of the game.": "End of an Era."

25   I have always left programs . . . TCU will be no different.: "End of an Era."

26   the team had only twenty . . . of the game were run: Don L. Wulffsen, "Unconscious Player Preserves TCU Victory," *Greatest Moments in TCU Football History*, p. 72.

26   It's the only time . . . won a football game.: Wulffsen, "Unconscious Player Preserves TCU Victory," *Greatest Moments in TCU Football History*, p. 72.

27   In the silence of a disappointed . . . move forward from there?": Gil LeBreton, "Foreword," *Believe It!* (Chicago: Triumph Books, 2011), p. 6.

27   To us, there was unfinished business.: LeBreton, "Foreword," *Believe It!*, p. 6.

28   "the toughest place to play in America": Gil LeBreton, ""Patterson's Preparation Served Frogs Well in Boise," *Star-Telegram.com*, Nov. 14, 2011, http://nl.newsbank.com/nl-search/we/Archives?p_action=doc&p_docid=13C37E199A431.

28   "didn't lose the game. . . . into Bronco Stadium and took it.": LeBreton, "Patterson's Preparation."

28   The Thursday afternoon before . . . task at hand was.: LeBreton, "Patterson's Preparation."

28   "cement[ed] his Mountain . . . grabbing for it all.": LeBreton, "Patterson's Preparation."

28   After the game, Patterson . . . "have thought of something.": LeBreton, "Patterson's Preparation."

28   That game was won . . . in the weeks and nights before it.: LeBreton, "Patterson's Preparation."

29   When the NCAA changed its . . . rather than a hobby: Wyatt Kanyer, "Support and Recruiting Characterize Coach's Career," *tcu360*, Nov. 23, 2012, http://www.tcu360.com/mens-golf/2012/11/16522.

29   He had gotten so good . . .decided to hire him.: Kanyer, "Support and Recruiting."

29   Montigel took the position . . . to play golf every day.: Max Montemer, "Trust, Experience Vital in Golf Coach's Recruiting Tactics," *tcu360*, April 22, 2013, http://www.tcu360.com/mens-golf/2013/04/17932.

29   We actually got beat . . . to be kidding me.: Montemer, "Trust, Experience Vital."

30   the players agreed before the . . . first quarter was the fourth.: Mike Jones, "Razorbacks Frog-Tied," *Greatest Moments in TCU Football History*, p. 202.

30   Maybe this removes any . . . comeback wins were flukes.: Mike Jones, "Razorbacks Frog-Tied," *Greatest Moments in TCU Football History*, p. 202.

31   Before he suited up for . . . his comeback from the injury.": Mark Wright, "Back in Business," *The TCU Magazine*, Spring 2008, http://www.magarchive.tcu.edu/articles/2008-01-RR4.asp.

31   My dad told me everything . . . look on the bright side.: Wright, "Back in Business."

32   his high school team in . . . called "college football's greatest passer: Whit Canning, "Sammy Baugh: College Football's Greatest Passer," *Greatest Moments in TCU Football History*, p. 62.

32   gained his proficiency by . . . often on the run.: "Sammy Baugh," *Wikipedia, the free encyclopedia*, http://en.wikipedia.org/wiki/Sammy_Baugh.

32   Baugh was actually viewed . . . out of high school.: Canning, "Sammy Baugh," *Greatest Moments in TCU Football History*, p. 62.

32   Meyer recruited Baugh . . . he could also play baseball.: Canning, "Sammy Baugh," *Greatest*

32 *Moments in TCU Football History*, p. 64.
32 a Texas sportswriter dubbed . . . not the gridiron.: "Sammy Baugh," *Wikipedia.*
32 Dutch [Meyer] recruited me for baseball with the idea that I could also play football.: Canning, "Sammy Baugh," *Greatest Moments in TCU Football History*, p. 64.
33 At halftime, the coaches told . . . win [the] game for him.": Clifford King and Pat Truly, "PIttman's Death Mars Win," *Greatest Moments in TCU Football History*, p. 178.
33 carried two defenders with him: King and Truly, *Greatest Moments in TCU Football History*, p. 179.
33 We wanted to win it for [Jim Pittman] and in his memory.: King and Truly, *Greatest Moments in TCU Football History*, p. 178.
34 One newspaper headline that . . . Meets Heir Apparent.": Whit Canning, "Memorial Stadium: Once TCU's Home on the Road," *Greatest Moments in TCU Football History*, p. 221.
34 slid through a hole . . . hit this hard all year.": Canning, "Memorial Stadium," *Greatest Moments in TCU Football History*, p. 221.
35 Tuohimaa had her life all . . . was there anything else?": Troy Phillips, "The Old College Try," *The TCU Magazine*, Summer 2010, http://www.magazine.tcu.edu/Magazine/Article. aspx?ArticleId=357.
35 she got in touch with . . . obtained a student visa.: Phillips, "The Old College Try."
35 "giving into Hammond's overtures . . . decision she ever made.: Phillips, "The Old College Try."
35 I chased her for two years. . . . until she got hold of us.: Phillips, "The Old College Try."
36 Ohio State's president chided . . . schedule of the Big Ten conference,: LeBreton, "Foreword," *Believe It!*, p. 8.
36 "13-0 is top of the mountain,": Stefan Stevenson, "TCU Finishes Perfect Season," *Believe It!*, p. 16.
36 The memories will be forever. LeBreton, "Foreword," Believe It!, p. 8.
37 Vaught wasn't sure that he . . . swerved to meet him.": Whit Canning, "TCU's All-SWC Line," *Greatest Moments in TCU Football History*, p. 44.
37 The other return man hit . . . recovered and played on,: Canning, "TCU's All-SWC Line," *Greatest Moments in TCU Football History*, p. 45.
37 [The] hit [on Johnny Vaught] . . . was still [remembered] 30 years later.: Canning, "TCU's All-SWC Line," *Greatest Moments in TCU Football History*, p. 45.
38 TCU rider Courtney Motz . . . completely willing and relaxed,": Morgan Welch, "Equestrian: Being Prepared for the Unexpected," *tcu360*, Dec. 5, 2012, http://www.tcu360.com/sports/2012/ 12/16637.
38 To Jacobi, Overtime, her favorite . . . definitely a team leader.": Taylor Prater, "Equestrian Horses Regarded as Teammates," *tcu360*, April 8, 2013, http://www.tcu360.com/sports/2013/04/17760.
38 They're teammates, not just horses.: Prater, "Equestrian Horses Regarded as Teammates."
39 On Labor Day 2009, Petta was . . . "Did he have red hair?" "Yes," Isabel said.: David Casstevens, "Her Dog Had Fallen Ill," *Star-Telegram.com*, Sept. 12, 2009, http://nl.newsbank.com/nl-search/we/Archives?p_action=doc&p_docid=12BC7DCE92CD9.
40 "They'd stop by the school . . . Division I scholarship athlete.: Dan Greene, "Getting Big -- and Into the Big Time," *Sports Illustrated*, Aug. 16, 2012, http://sportsillustrated.cnn.com/vault/article/ magazine/MAG1203470/index.htm.
40 He was a leader . . . to keep his weight down.: Greene, "Getting Big."
40 A lot of people told me I can't do stuff. I just kind of use it as my fuel.: Greene, "Getting Big."
41 His collection of basketball sneakers . . . when he was at TCU.: Rick Waters, "Getting His Kicks," *The TCU Magazine*, Winter 2007, http://www.magarchive.tcu.edu/articles/2007-04-RR4.asp.
41 He could recite from memory . . . to find the best deals.": Waters, "Getting His Kicks."
41 he switched his jersey number to change his luck: Waters, "Getting His Kicks."
41 Definitely more [shoes] than I have matching clothes to go with them.: Waters, "Getting His Kicks."
42 representatives from the Orange, Rose, and Fiesta bowls,: "No. 4 TCU Crushes No. 16 Utah, 55-28," *cstv.com*, Nov. 14, 2009, http://www.cstv.com/printable/schools/tcu/sports/m-footbl/recaps.
42 they stormed the field when the game was over.: "No. 4 TCU Crushes No. 16 Utah."
42 The Frogs put on quite a show.: "No. 4 TCU Crushes No. 16 Utah."
43 After the 1940 season, . . . singed a contract for $4,500.: Elston Brooks, "Hollywood a Baugh for Slingin' Sammy," *Greatest Moments in TCU Football History*, p. 69.
43 The movie turned out to be . . . his six weeks on the set,: Brooks, "Hollywood a Baugh for Slingin' Sammy," *Greatest Moments in TCU Football History*, p. 68.
43 Baugh rubbed elbows with some . . . Tom Steele, and Pauline Moore,: Brooks, "Hollywood a Baugh for Slingin' Sammy," *Greatest Moments in TCU Football History*, p. 69.
43 the first day on the set . . . I was ready or not.": Brooks, "Hollywood a Baugh for Slingin' Sammy," *Greatest Moments in TCU Football History*, p. 69.
43 I can recall no other . . . I spent on that picture.: Brooks, "Hollywood a Baugh for Slingin' Sammy," *Greatest Moments in TCU Football History*, p. 69.

44 "No hits, no long runs, no errors, no bruises.": Galen Wlkins, "Butterflies Aside, Freshman Frog Turns in Exceptional Game," *Greatest Moments in TCU Football History*, p. 200.

44 "a player whose feet were not damp, much less wet.": Wlkins, "Butterflies Aside," *Greatest Moments in TCU Football History*, p. 200.

44 with 1:03 left in the . . . his face really lit up.": Wilkins, "Butterflies Aside," *Greatest Moments in TCU Football History*, p. 200.

44 "[Leon] Clay never knew . . . looked good on him.": Wilkins, "Butterflies Aside," *Greatest Moments in TCU Football History*, p. 201.

44 Big Butterflies. The biggest I've felt since my first game in high school.: Wilkins, "Butterflies Aside," *Greatest Moments in TCU Football History*, p. 200.

45 When Cannon was 15, . . . he finished his chemo: Charean Williams, "'Your Reason to Believe,'" *Star-Telegram.com*, July 3, 2011, http://nl.newsbank.com/nl-search/we/Archives?p_action= doc&p_docid=13840867ABBD.

45 All I can do is keep . . . and accept my healing.: Williams, " Your Reason to Believe.'"

46 "a gaudy preseason ranking . . . little more than halfhearted.: Rick Waters, "From Kicked Out to Kick-Started," *The TCU Magazine*, Fall 2010, http://www.magazine.tcu.edu/Magazine/ Article.aspx?ArticleId=414.

46 The head coach kicked the . . . we're practicing,'": Waters, "From Kicked Out to Kick-Started."

46 We needed a jolt to . . . what we would have done.: Waters, "From Kicked Out to Kick-Started."

47 the unimproved field on which . . . influenced the decision: Nancy Bartosek, "Frog of Ages," *The TCU Magazine*, Fall 2001, http://www.magarchive.tcu.edu/articles/2001-03-CV3.asp.

47 "the apex of intimidation.": "TCU's New Horned Frog Is the Apex of Intimidation," *bigleadsports*, March 24, 2013, http://www.thebiglead.com/index.php/2013/03/24/tcus-new-horned-frog.

48 hoping for a shot at being named . . . sure we have the right guy?": Rick Waters, "Making His Own Legend," *The TCU Magazine*, Fall 2012, http://www.magazine.tcu.edu/Magazine/ Article.aspx?ArticleId=713.

48 He's been remarkable for . . . record speaks for itself.: Waters, "Making His Own Legend."

49 The forecast for TCU's . . . temperatures in the 80s.: Whit Canning, "Frogs Edged in 'The Hurricane Game,'" *Greatest Moments in TCU Football History*, p. 136.

49 "Strangest game I ever . . . we had a tornado.": Canning, "Frogs Edged in 'The Hurricane Game,'" *Greatest Moments in TCU Football History*, p. 137.

49 half of the capacity crowd "had fled in terror.": Canning, "Frogs Edged in 'The Hurricane Game,'" *Greatest Moments in TCU Football History*, p. 136.

49 he'd call the signals . . . bouncing off their helmets.": Canning, "Frogs Edged in 'The Hurricane Game,'" *Greatest Moments in TCU Football History*, p. 137.

49 All-American halfback Jim . . . all over his glasses,": Canning, "Frogs Edged in 'The Hurricane Game,'" *Greatest Moments in TCU Football History*, p. 137.

49 You had to turn your head to breathe.: Canning, "Frogs Edged in 'The Hurricane Game,'" *Greatest Moments in TCU Football History*, p. 137.

50 When she was being recruited . . . the golf program's structure.: Kristin Barnes, "Rutgers Transfer Finds Home," *tcu360*, April 13, 2013, http://www.tcu360.com/womens-golf/2013/04/17831.

50 "She came to us," . . . calms me down on the course.": Barnes, "Rutgers Transfer Finds Home."

50 The program here is more . . . which I thrive off of.: Barnes, "Rutgers Transfer Finds Home."

51 When the TCU football . . . "I have always loved football,": Brent Yarina, "Former Soccer Player Emerges as Strong Kicker," *TCU Daily Skiff*, Aug. 29, 2003, http://www.skiff.tcu.edu/ fall2003/082903/formhtml.

51 "because I was on a . . . "Who?" Patterson asked.: Damien Pierce, "Kicker Browne Is TCU's Point Man," *Star-Telegram.com*, Oct. 23, 2003, http://nl.newsbank.com/nl-search/we/Archives?p_ action=doc&p_docid=0FGE7798F1FA3E.

51 Wow, I didn't expect that!: Pierce, "Kicker Browne Is TCU's Point Man."

52 "the most memorable Thanksgiving . . . played in the game.: Gil LeBreton, "TCU's Patterson Takes Victory in Stride," *Star-Telegram.com*, Nov. 23, 2012, http://nl.newsbank.com/nl-search/we/ Archives?p_action=doc&p_docid=142BCECC06FC.

52 He said that if he proclaimed . . . a lot of ballgames like this.": LeBreton, "TCU's Patterson Takes Victory in Stride."

52 Boykin "stole the night's show.": LeBreton, "TCU's Patterson Takes Victory in Stride."

52 With only five minutes to play, . . . 200 yards of total offense.: LeBreton, "TCU's Patterson Takes Victory in Stride."

53 Aug. 25, the date of his . . . come together to celebrate,": Greg Riddle, "World-Class Speed," *The TCU Magazine*, Winter 2003, http://www.magarchive.tcu.edu/article/2003-04-RR.asp? issue-id=200304.

53 This is the biggest thing that ever happened to the island.: Riddle, "World-Class Speed."

54   Patterson admitted he was . . . way we needed to,": "Frogs Rout In-State Rival Bobcats, 56-21."
       GoFrogs.com, Sept. 19, 2009. http://www.cstv.com/printable/schools/tcu/sports/m-footbl/
       recaps/091909.aab.html.

54   "We have to have attention . . . to be what we want to be.": "Frogs Rout In-State Rival."

54   It will be good for us, will get us to focus more.: "Frogs Rout In-State Rival."

55   Prior to the game . . . burning some 40,000 red candles.: Flem Hall, "Swink Stampedes for 4 Scores,
       Frogs Win, 47-20," *Greatest Moments in TCU Football History*, p. 128.

55   "in one of the most brilliant one-man shows in conference history.": Flem Hall, "Swink Stampedes
       for 4 Scores, Frogs Win, 47-20," *Greatest Moments in TCU Football History*, p. 128.

55   "putting on the largest . . . marshalled against the Longhorns.": Flem Hall, "Swink Stampedes for 4
       Scores, Frogs Win, 47-20," *Greatest Moments in TCU Football History*, p. 128.

55   All week, thousands of Longhorn . . . to overcome formidable foes.: Flem Hall, "Swink Stampedes
       for 4 Scores, Frogs Win, 47-20," *Greatest Moments in TCU Football History*, p. 128.

56   "There were a lot of times . . . right into my arms.": Whit Canning, "Davey O'Brien All He Did Was
       Win," *Greatest Moments in TCU Football History*, p. 84.

56   "was one of the first players . . . away from his friends.": Whit Canning, "Davey O'Brien: All He
       Did Was Win," *Greatest Moments in TCU Football History*, p. 82.

56   I never thought of . . . And he was tough.: Whit Canning, "Davey O'Brien: All He Did Was Win,"
       Greatest Moments in TCU Football History, p. 81.

57   In the fall of 1974, . . . to play an 8 a.m. game.: Bob Frye, "First Ladies," *The TCU Magazine*, Summer
       2001, http://www.magarchive.tcu.edu/articles/2001-02-RRasp?issueid=200102.

57   I frequently looked up from . . . total, in the stands.: Frye, "First Ladies."

58   The player KILLERFROGS.com named . . . (behind Mike Renfro): Ed Kamen, "TCU Football: The
       Best of the Best -- Receiver," *KILLERFROGS.com*, March 13, 2012, http://www.killerfrogs.
       com/msgboard/index.php?showtopic=152338.

58   "We need those magic hands . . . started to get that feeling,": David Moore, "TCU's Washington
       Finds the Magic," *Greatest Moments in TCU Football History*, p. 180.

58   Washington lined up at . . . just a matter of hitting him,": Moore, "TCU''s Washington," *Greatest
       Moments in TCU Football History*, pp. 180-81.

58   I got the feeling that if I . . . get it into the end zone.: Moore, "TCU''s Washington," *Greatest Moments
       in TCU Football History*, p. 180.

59   hadn't played a down since the Baylor game three weeks before: Dick Moore, "Punt Return by
       Thornton Ignites TCU," *Greatest Moments in TCU Football History*, p. 174.

59   safety Mike Hall had yelled . . . then followed his blockers: Moore, "Punt Return by Thornton,"
       Greatest Moments in TCU Football History, p. 175.

59   "Don't give me credit," . . . "Give it to the blockers.": Moore, "Punt Return by Thornton," *Greatest
       Moments in TCU Football History*, p. 174.

59   "You could feel something . . . sweeping through everyone.": Moore, "Punt Return by Thornton,"
       Greatest Moments in TCU Football History, p. 174.

59   That gave us the momentum.: Moore, "Punt Return by Thornton," *Greatest Moments in TCU Football
       History*, p. 174.

60   When the Southwest Conference . . . "abandoned on the doorstep,": LeBreton, "Foreword," *Believe
       It!*, p. 8.

60   "the tragedy of coach . . . handed to it in 1986.": LeBreton, "Foreword," *Believe It!*, p. 8.

60   "It took so long . . . And we're here. It's unbelievable.": Gil LeBreton, "The Frogs Are Deserving
       Rose Bowl Champions," *Believe It!*, p. 20.

60   In the locker room, head coach . . . Network authenticity failed.": LeBreton, "The Frogs Are Deserv-
       ing Rose Bowl Champions," *Believe It!*, p. 26.

60   One of college football's . . . unique and glorious chapter.: "The Frogs Are Deserving Rose Bowl
       Champions," *Believe It!*, p. 26.

61   Despite sending e-mails to . . . He named Cole.: Max Montemer, "Golfer Plans to Improve His
       Game," *tcu360*, April 29, 2013, http://www.tcu360.com/mens-golf/2013/04/18011.

61   he broke his leg in . . . that most players overlook: Montemer, "Golfer Plans to Improve His Game."

61   Montigel called Cole's injury . . . "made his game a lot better,": Montemer, "Golfer Plans to Improve
       His Game."

61   I took that period . . . needed to do better.: Montemer, "Golfer Plans to Improve His Game."

62   "I felt like Tye would start all 11 games and play well the entire year,": Rick Waters, "Another
       Off-the-Bench Hero," *The TCU Magazine*, Winter 2005, http://www.magarchive.tcu.edu/
       articles/2005-04-rr.asp?issueid=200504.

62   "I'm still surprised to see . . . and watch the tape,": Waters, "Another Off-the-
       Bench Hero."

62   "In truth," . . . saved the Frogs' season.": Waters, "Another Off-the-Bench Hero."

62 I didn't expect this season . . . . Not in a million years.: Waters, "Another Off-the Bench Hero."

63 In August 2005, Hurricane Katrina . . . and how they interacted,": Stefan Stevenson, "Head of the Family Kenny Cain Draws on Toughness," *Star-Telegram.com*, Sept. 29, 2012, http:// nl.newsbank.com/nl-search/we/Archives?p_action=doc&p_docid=141B2A831FBF7.

63 "ambivalent, vacillating, impulsive, unsubmissive.": MacArthur, *Twelve Ordinary Men*, p. 39.

63 "the greatest preacher among . . . birth of the church.: MacArthur, *Twelve Ordinary Men*, p. 39.

63 Cain's teammates look to him for guidance and strength.: Stevenson, "Head of the Family Kenny Cain Draws on Toughness."

64 "nearly found out what life is like at the other end of the rock.": Gil LeBreton, "TCU Wakes Up in Time," *Star-Telegram.com*, Dec. 22, 2011, http://nl.newsbank.com/nl-search/we/Archives?p_action=doc&p_docid=13BCBC6ABAF.

64 a program accustomed to . . . collective pulse raised: LeBreton, "TCU Wakes Up in Time."

64 That performance left head . . . changed the signals at halftime.: Stefan Stevenson, "Second-Half Turnaround Sparked TCU," *Star-Telegram.com*, Dec. 23, 2011, http://nl.newsbank.com/nl-search/we/Archives?p_action=doc&p_docid=13BD10F2079888.

64 If they have the same . . . not doing their job.: Stevenson, "Second-Half Turnaround Sparked TCU."

65 he tweeted before a game . . . the court in college.: Stefan Stevenson, "Thorns Scores 32," *Star-Telegram.com*, Feb. 15, 2012, http://nl.newsbank.com/nl-search/we/Archives?p_action=doc&p_docid=13DF7E969D4A.

65 "a sizzling, singular performance." . . . in recent TCU history.": Stevenson, "Thorns Scores 32."

65 The Rebs led at halftime . . . layup started the OT: Stevenson, "Thorns Scores 32."

65 When the buzzer sounded, . . . who had stormed the court.: Stevenson, "Thorns Scores 32."

65 I was hot; I can't explain it. I was feeling it.: Stevenson, "Thorns Scores 32."

66 The Horned Frogs played "as glorious a game as ever a TCU team turned in": Flem Hall, "Frogs Win National Title," *Greatest Moments in TCU Football History*, p. 56.

66 Heavy rains for three days . . . a "veritable morass.": Hall, "Frogs Win National Title," *Greatest Moments in TCU Football History*, p. 56.

66 a cold wind that "swept the rain in slanting sheets across the field,": Hall, "Frogs Win National Title," *Greatest Moments in TCU Football History*, p. 56.

66 snapped the wet, slick, heavy ball perfectly.: Hall, "Frogs Win National Title," *Greatest Moments in TCU Football History*, p. 57.

66 Ordinarily, mud battles are . . . in this Sugar Bowl scrap.: Hall, "Frogs Win National Title," *Greatest Moments in TCU Football History*, p. 57.

67 "We did believe,": "TCU 28, USC 19," *SI.com*, Dec. 31, 1998, http://sportsillustrated.cnn.com/football/college/scoreboards/1998/12/31/recap.tcu.usc.html.

67 We might have been the only . . . we could beat [the Trojans].: "TCU 28, USC 19."

68 "threw the heck out of it.": Whit Canning, "Memorial Stadium: Once TCU's Home on the Road," *Greatest Moments in TCU Football History*, p. 223.

68 "Buddy actually landed . . . over the goal line.: Canning, "Memorial Stadium," *Greatest Moments in TCU Football History*, p. 223.

68 He spent years trying to . . . fall into and mess up.": Canning, "Memorial Stadium," *Greatest Moments in TCU Football History*, p. 220.

68 I've tried to tell him that his . . . doesn't see it that way.: Canning, "Memorial Stadium," *Greatest Moments in TCU Football History*, p. 220.

69 "Baseball is crazy.": Stefan Stevenson, "TCU Recovers from 11-Run Meltdown to Scrape Win in Ninth," *Star-Telegram.com*, May 25, 2012, http://nl.newsbank.com/nl-search/we/Archives?p_action=doc&p_docid=13EFCF0629BB2.

69 "A Frogs victory was considered a foregone conclusion": Stevenson, "TCU Recovers."

69 "It just kept getting . . . it out of [their] grasp,": Stevenson, "TCU Recovers."

69 That's the most ridiculous game I've ever been part of.: Stevenson, "TCU Recovers."

70 the team's fastest player: Johnny Paul, "TCU Claims a Share of Title," *Greatest Moments in TCU Football History*, p. 215.

70 "This is up to you guys. . . . fall on my shoulders.": Paul, "TCU Claims a Share of Title," *Greatest Moments in TCU Football History*, p. 214.

70 They needed something they . . . now they've got it.: Paul, "TCU Claims a Share of Title," *Greatest Moments in TCU Football History*, p. 214.

71 Not until the basketball season . . . 65 yards for a touchdown.: Whit Canning, "Swink Ruled the Southwest," *Greatest Moments in TCU Football History*, p. 144.

71 behind a block from end . . . keep up with him, anyway.": Canning, "Swink Rules the Southwest," *Greatest Moments in TCU Football History*, p. 145.

72 His folks dubbed their newest . . . months after his birth.: "Tank Carder," *Wikipedia, the free encyclopedia*, en.wikipedia.org/wiki/Tank_Carder.

72   Ricky was 13 when he . . . until his sophomore year.: Stefan Stevenson, "Tank Driven to Succeed," *Star-Telegram.com*, Oct. 24, 2009, http://nl.newsbank.com/nl-search/we/Archives?p_action=doc&p_docid=12B9D6BCF884A.

72   Tank has got more . . . anybody I've ever met.: Stevenson, "Tank Driven to Succeed."

73   When she was in the second . . . an AAU team that spring.: Paul Kix, "Alone No More," *Dallas Observer*, March 31, 2005, http://www.dallasobserver.com/2005-03-31/news/alone-no-more.

73   Dear Coach. I will improve my game. We will never lose again.: Kix, "Alone No More."

74   Because of the great . . . an insignificant red dot.": Dick Moore, "Meyer Built a Winner," *Greatest Moments in TCU Football History*, p. 126.

74   "the most cherished sports prize of all in the 1930s": Moore, "Meyer Built a Winner," *Greatest Moments in TCU Football History*, p. 126.

74   "I just laid my head down in the press box and cried,": Moore, "Meyer Built a Winner," *Greatest Moments in TCU Football History*, p. 126.

74   In New York for . . . shoot for in future seasons.: Moore, "Meyer Built a Winner," *Greatest Moments in TCU Football History*, p. 127.

75   Martin himself welcomed visitors . . . if that isn't its purpose.": Gene Gregston, "Cool Coach of the Horned Frogs," *Greatest Moments in TCU Football History*, p. 166.

75   "I think athletic personnel . . . of the English department,": Gregston, "Cool Coach of the Horned Frogs," *Greatest Moments in TCU Football History*, p. 170.

75   Funds raised by the . . . coach a bunch of coaches.": Gregston, "Cool Coach of the Horned Frogs," *Greatest Moments in TCU Football History*, p. 171.

75   [TCU] has the most sensible approach to athletics of any in the major-college field.: Gregston, "Cool Coach of the Horned Frogs," *Greatest Moments in TCU Football History*, p. 171.

76   The school's star javelin thrower . . . separate good from great.": Rick Waters, "Borrowed Brilliance," *The TCU Magazine*, Winter 2008, http://www.magarchive.tcu.edu/articles/2008-03-RR3.asp.

76   If you know how to use it, a superior javelin will reward you.: Waters, "Borrowed Brilliance."

77   "My mom and my brother . . . model and surrogate father.: "In the Hunt," *The TCU Magazine*, Fall 1999, http://www.magarchive.tcu.edu/articles/1999-03-RR.asp?issueid=199903.

77   Washington introduced Hunt to football . . . home during the holidays.": "In the Hunt."

77   "He was my inspiration," . . . switched to football.: "In the Hunt."

77   because that was where Washington had played.: "Meet the Reaper -- Reggie Hunt," *GregorHutton.com*, http://www.gregorhutton.com/reggiehunt/index3.html.

77   "following in [his cousin's] unfinished footsteps.": "In the Hunt."

77   [Reggie] Hunt's arm says it . . . and then below it: 1967-1990.: "In the Hunt."

78   Matthews enrolled briefly at . . . there were no women.": Whit Canning, "TCU's First All-American," *Greatest Moments in TCU Football History*, p. 39.

78   "a good receiver and an absolute terror on defense.": Whit Canning, "TCU's First All-American," *Greatest Moments in TCU Football History*, p. 38.

78   the A&M huddle was rudely . . . it was Matthews.: Whit Canning, "TCU's First All-American," *Greatest Moments in TCU Football History*, p. 38.

78   Matthews then stepped across . . . Here I come.": Whit Canning, "TCU's First All-American," *Greatest Moments in TCU Football History*, p. 38.

78   I always did some talking out on the field.: Whit Canning, "TCU's First All-American," *Greatest Moments in TCU Football History*, p. 38.

79   Andy Dalton's receivers dropped four passes on TCU's first possession,: Stefan Stevenson, "The Defense Shines," *Believe It!*, p. 68.

79   just before the second-half . . . "Play like it.": Stevenson, "The Defense Shines," *Believe It!*, p. 66.

79   behind a block from fullback Luke Shivers: Stevenson, "The Defense Shines," *Believe It!*, p. 70.

79   block from All-American tackle Marcus Cannon: Stevenson, "The Defense Shines," *Believe It!*, p. 70.

80   Edwards admitted that her . . . "to keep making her proud.": Rick Waters, "Inspired by Family," *The TCU Magazine*, Winter 2009, http://www.magazine.tcu.edu/Magazine/Article.aspx?ArticleId=260.

80   I know [my mom . . . "I know that for sure.": Waters, "Inspired by Family."

80   I know she's watching me and cheering me on.: Waters, "Inspired by Family."

81   The number on his practice . . . after a redshirt season.: Austin Murphy, "Horned Frog Formula," *Sports Illustrated*, Oct. 12, 2009, http://sportsillustrated.cnn.com/vault/article/magazine/MAG1161009/index.htm.

81   As he left the office, . . . is this going to work?": Murphy, "Horned Frog Formula."

81   All this is much more than we expected. We didn't see this coming at all.: Murphy, "Horned Frog Formula."

82   in the first quarter of the . . . him to the locker room,: Stevenson, "Williamson Not Afraid," *Believe It!*, p. 116.

82   when his wife, Patty, came in, . . . and we were praying for our dad,": Stevenson, "Williamson Not Afraid," *Believe It!*, p. 118.

82   "The one thing I found out . . . not afraid to die, either.": Stevenson, "Williamson Not Afraid," *Believe It!*, p. 119.

82   I am a person of faith. I'm not afraid to die, but I didn't want to.: Stevenson, "Williamson Not Afraid," *Believe It!*, p. 116.

83   Lawrence had apparently been . . . and took it in.: Flem Hall, "Frogs Knock Owls Off Unbeaten Roost," *Greatest Moments in TCU Football History*, pp. 46-47.

83   knocked the offending official . . . squad of policemen showed up.: Hall, "Frogs Knock Owls Off Unbeaten Roost," *Greatest Moments in TCU Football History*, p. 47.

83   There was a great deal . . . finally cleared the gridiron.: Hall, "Frogs Knock Owls Off Unbeaten Roost," *Greatest Moments in TCU Football History*, p. 47.

84   "a memorable player who . . . else down the road.": Tracey Myers, "Women's Insider: Dziuk a Pioneer for TCU Women," *Star-Telegram.com*, Oct. 7, 2002, http://nl.newsbank.com/nl-search/we/Archives?p_action=doc&p_docid=0F689772E19A375.

84   She really did lay a . . . basketball players to follow.: Myers, "Women's Insider."

85   "This game is going to tell . . . and lose this game.": Stefan Stevenson, "For National Prestige, It's One Big Game for Frogs," *Star-Telegram.com*, Sept. 26, 2009, http://nl.newsbank.com/nl-search/we/Archives?p_action=doc&p_docid=12AF9DF343C90E

85   the AD offered TCU . . . it was a win.": Drew Davison, "TCU Horned Frogs [*sic*] Trip to Clemson's Death Valley Was Defining Detour," *Star-Telegram.com*, Dec. 20, 2009, http://nl.newsbank.com/nl-search/we/Archives?p_action=doc&p_docid=12CB79FA2C252.

85   this "pedigreed opponent": Gil LeBreton, "Knowing All About Scary, TCU Feared Not Valley of Death," *Star-Telegram.com*, Sept. 27, 2009, http://nl.newsbank.com/nl-search/we/Archives?p_action=doc&p_docid=12B09CD0309F6E.

85   The screams of about . . . a silent snap count.: Stefan Stevenson, "Frogs Rain on Clemson Parade," *Star-Telegram.com*, Sept. 27, 2009, http://nl.newsbank.com/nl-search/we/Archives?p_action=doc&p_docid=12B09CD0382492.

85   like they feared nothing, . . . the better of them.": LeBreton, "Knowing All About Scary."

85   "with confidence on . . . among the heavy raindrops.": Stevenson, "Frogs Rain on Clemson Parade."

85   "the kind of aggressive . . . makes on the road.": Stevenson, "Frogs Rain on Clemson Parade."

85   We gained a lot of confidence as a football team.: LeBreton, "Knowing All About Scary."

86   her brother "is always with me. He's a part of who I am.": Gil LeBreton, "With Dislocated Elbow, TCU Shooter Shows Her Tough Side," *Star-Telegram*, July 29, 2012. http://www.star-telegram.com/2012/07/29/4134408/with-dislocated-elbow-tcu-shooter.html.

86   Only five days before . . . shooting through her elbow.: LeBreton, "With Dislocated Elbow."

86   Sarah is tough. She has self-control. She's a tough young lady.: LeBreton, "With Dislocated Elbow."

87   "and effectively turned it into a series of soapbox opportunities.": Ray Buck, "Gary Patterson," *Believe It!*, p. 30.

87   giving him what they call . . . assortment of bobbleheads.": Buck, "Gary Patterson," *Believe It!*, p. 30.

87   Then it was on to *First Take* . . . in an overstuffed chair.: Buck, "Gary Patterson," *Believe It!*, p. 32.

87   After his last appearance . . . hopped a jet to Chicago.: Buck, "Gary Patterson," *Believe It!*, p. 30.

87   I'm here [because] I owe . . . stage in college football.: Buck, "Gary Patterson," *Believe It!*, p. 32.

88   "college football's greatest defensive tackle,": *Greatest Moments in TCU Football History*, p. 158.

88   "we were sputtering offensively,": Whit Canning, "Members of '59 TCU Team Recall Their Trip to 1st Bluebonnet Bowl," *Greatest Moments in TCU Football History*, p. 156.

88   the head coach asked . . . he took their advice.: Canning, "Members of '59 TCU Team Recall Their Trip to 1st Bluebonnet Bowl," *Greatest Moments in TCU Football History*, p. 156.

88   "There was a special feeling . . . no one could stop us.: Canning, "Members of '59 TCU Team Recall Their Trip to 1st Bluebonnet Bowl," *Greatest Moments in TCU Football History*, p. 156.

88   If we'd gone with Jackie . . . could've really been something.: Canning, "Members of '59 TCU Team Recall Their Trip to 1st Bluebonnet Bowl," *Greatest Moments in TCU Football History*, p. 157.

89   "We've got mostly 210- to . . . yards of offense per game.: Mike Heika, "Big 'D' at TCU," *Greatest Moments in TCU Football History*, p. 209.

89   End Junji Bolden fought off . . . showed guts and character," Heika, "Big 'D' at TCU," *Greatest Moments in TCU Football History*, p. 209.

89   "The key to this victory was heart,": Mike Jones, "Shocker: TCU 23, Texas 14," *Greatest Moments in TCU Football History*, p. 206.

89   Our coaches convinced us we could win if we play 'guts out' football.: Heika, "Big 'D' at TCU," *Greatest Moments in TCU Football History*, p. 209.

90   "looks like a goofball . . . was "an unbeatable assassin.": Brian Bennett, "Indomitable Purke
      Powers Horned Frogs," *ESPN.com*, June 25, 2010, http://sports.espn.go.com/ncaa/news/
      story?id=5329768.
90   Bryan Holaday trotted to . . . and do your thing.": David Ubben, "Purke Stymies Seminoles in CWS
      Opener," *ESPN.com*, June 19, 2010, http://espn.go.com/ncaa/blog/_/name/ncaa_baseball/
      id/5306296.
90   The more that he's cornered, the better that he is.: Ubben, "Purke Stymies Seminoles."
91   Prior to the 1946 game, . . . brought to the table.": Molly Mahan and Rick Waters, "The History of
      the Iron Skillet," *The TCU Magazine*, Fall 2009, http://www.magazine.tcu.edu/Magazine/
      Article.aspx?Articleid=199.
91   An old story claims that . . . legs were handed over.: "Battle for the Iron Skillet," *Wikipedia, the free
      encyclopedia*, http://en.wikipedia.org/wiki/Battle_for_the_iron_skillet.
92   Two weeks before August camp . . . Deck readily agreed.: Stefan Stevenson, "TCU Senior Deck
      Finds New Home at Right Tackle," *Star-Telegram.com*, Oct. 19, 2011, http://nl.newsbank.com/
      nl-search/we/Archives?p_action=doc&p_docid=13A7A0E74BF54.
92   he made a "mockery out . . . to accommodate Deck.: Stefan Stevenson, "Frogs' Tight End Quickly
      Turns Into Starting Offensive Tackle," *Star-Telegram.com*, Sept. 1, 2011, http://nl.newsbank.
      com/nl-search/we/Archives?p_action=doc&p_docid=1397CEE46297C.
92   "He's cooking all the . . . pulls out of the oven,": Stevenson, "TCU Senior Deck Finds New Home."
92   The other day we . . . killed three pork roasts.: Stevenson, "TCU Senior Deck Finds New Home."

BIBLIOGRAPHY

Barnes, Kristen. "Rutgers Transfer Finds Home on Women's Golf Team." *tcu360*. 13 April
    2013. http://www.tcu360.com/womens-golf/2013/04/17831.
Bartosek, Nancy. "Frog of Ages." *The TCU Magazine*. Fall 2001 . http://www.magarchive.tcu.
    edu/articles/2001-03-CV3.asp.
"Battle for the Iron Skillet." *Wikipedia, the free encyclopedia*. http://en.wikipedia.org/wiki/
    Battle_for_the_iron_skillet.
Bennett, Brian. "Frogs Drawn to a Rally." *ESPN.com*. 23 June 2010. http://sports.espn.go.
    com/ncaa/news/story?id=5321590.
-----. "Indomitable Purke Powers Horned Frogs." *ESPN.com*. 25 June 2010. http://sports.
    espn.go.com/ncaa/news/story?id=5329768.
---. "'Locked-In' Andy Dalton Finds Redemption." *ESPN.com*. 1 Jan. 2011. http://espn.go.
    com/blog/NCFNation/post/_/id/36923/locked-in-andy-dalton-finds-redemption.
-----. "Tank Carder in Right Place, Time for TCU." *ESPN.com*. 1 Jan. 2011. http://espn.go.
    com/blog/NCFNation/post/_/id36943/tank-carder-in-right-place-time-for-tcu.
Brooks, Elston. "Hollywood a Baugh for Slingin' Sammy." *Greatest Moments in TCU Football
    History*. Dan Jenkins and Francis J. Fitzgerald, eds. Louisville, Kent.: AdCraft Sports
    Marketing, 1996. 68-69.
Buck, Ray. "Gary Patterson: TCU Coach Takes to the National Airwaves to Make Case
    for Frogs." *Believe It! Rose Bowl Wins Caps TCU's Perfect Season*. Chicago: Triumph
    Books, 2011. 30, 32.
Canning, Whit. "Berry Outduels Walker in Final Meeting." *Greatest Moments in TCU Foot-
    ball History*. Dan Jenkins and Francis J. Fitzgerald, eds. Louisville, Kent.: AdCraft
    Sports Marketing, 1996. 110-11.
-----. "Davey O'Brien: All He Did Was Win." *Greatest Moments in TCU Foot-
    ball History*. Dan Jenkins and Francis J. Fitzgerald, eds. Louisville,

Kent.: AdCraft Sports Marketing, 1996. 79-85.

-----. "Frogs Edged in 'The Hurricane Game.'" *Greatest Moments in TCU Football History.* Dan Jenkins and Francis J. Fitzgerald, eds. Louisville, Kent.: AdCraft Sports Marketing, 1996. 136-37.

---. "Members of '59 TCU Team Recall Their Trip to 1st Bluebonnet Bowl." *Greatest Moments in TCU Football History.* Dan Jenkins and Francis J. Fitzgerald, eds. Louisville, Kent.: AdCraft Sports Marketing, 1996. 155-57.

-----. "Memorial Stadium: Once TCU's Home on the Road." *Greatest Moments in TCU Football History.* Dan Jenkins and Francis J. Fitzgerald, eds. Louisville, Kent.: AdCraft Sports Marketing, 1996. 220-223.

-----. "Sammy Baugh: College Football's Greatest Passer." *Greatest Moments in TCU Football History.* Dan Jenkins and Francis J. Fitzgerald, eds. Louisville, Kent.: AdCraft Sports Marketing, 1996. 62-67.

-----. Swink Ruled the Southwest." *Greatest Moments in TCU Football History.* Dan Jenkins and Francis J. Fitzgerald, eds. Louisville, Kent.: AdCraft Sports Marketing, 1996. 142-145.

-----. "TCU Upsets Sixth-ranked Texas A&M." *Greatest Moments in TCU Football History.* Dan Jenkins and Francis J. Fitzgerald, eds. Louisville, Kent.: AdCraft Sports Marketing, 1996. 112-13.

-----. "TCU's All-SWC Line." *Greatest Moments in TCU Football History.* Dan Jenkins and Francis J. Fitzgerald, eds. Louisville, Kent.: AdCraft Sports Marketing, 1996. 44-45.

-----. "TCU's First All-American." *Greatest Moments in TCU Football History.* Dan Jenkins and Francis J. Fitzgerald, eds. Louisville, Kent.: AdCraft Sports Marketing, 1996. 38-39.

Casstevens, David. "Her Dog Had Fallen Ill When a Famous Stranger Came to Help." *Star-Telegram.com.* 12 Sept. 2009. http://nl.newsbank.com/nl-search/we/Archives?p_action=doc&p_docid=12BC7DCE92CD9.

Davison, Drew. "TCU Horned Frogs [*sic*] Trip to Clemson's Death Valley Was Defining Detour." *Star-Telegram.com.* 20 Dec. 2009. http://nl.newsbank.com/nl-search/we/Archives?p_action=doc&p_docid=12CB79FA2C252.

Drape, Joe. "Assembling More Than a Football Program at T.C.U." *The New York Times.* 27 Aug. 2011. http://www.nytimes.com/2011/08/28/sportrs/ncaafootball/at-tcu-the-football-coach-Gary-Patterson.

"End of an Era." *The TCU Magazine.* Winter 2001. http://www.magarchive.tcu/edu/articles/2001-04-RR.asp?.

Engel, Mac. "TCU's KO of KU, Though Not Pretty, Is Something to Admire." *Star-Telegram.com.* 7 Feb. 2013. http://nl.newsbank.com/nl-search/we/Archives?p_action=doc&p_docid=144DB5FF7D55.

"First Game, First Victory." *Greatest Moments in TCU Football History.* Dan Jenkins and Francis J. Fitzgerald, eds. Louisville, Kent.: AdCraft Sports Marketing, 1996. 27.

"Freshman Jackson Leads TCU to 17-7 Comeback Victory over Baylor." GoFrogs.cstv.com. 3 Sept. 2006. http://www.gofrogs.cstv.com/m-footbl/recaps/090306aaa.html.

"Frogs Rout In-State Rival Bobcats, 56-21." *GoFrogs.com.* 19 Sept. 2009. http://www.cstv.com/printable/schools/tcu/sports/m-footbl/recaps/091909.aab.html.

Frye, Bob. "First Ladies." *The TCU Magazine.* Summer 2001. http://www.magarchive.tcu.edu/articles/2001-02-RR.asp?issueid=200102.

Greene, Dan. "Getting Big -- and Into The Big Time." *Sports Illustrated.* 16 Aug. 2012. http://sportsillustrated.cnn.com/vault/article/magazine/MAG1203470/index.htm.

Gregston, Gene. "Cool Coach of the Horned Frogs." *Greatest Moments in TCU Football History.* Dan Jenkins and Francis J. Fitzgerald, eds. Louisville, Kent.: AdCraft Sports Marketing, 1996. 166-71.

Hall, Flem. "Frogs Knock Owls Off Unbeaten Roost." *Greatest Moments in TCU Football History.* Dan Jenkins and Francis J. Fitzgerald, eds. Louisville, Kent.: AdCraft

198

Sports Marketing, 1996. 46-47.

-----. "Frogs Win National Title." *Greatest Moments in TCU Football History.* Dan Jenkins and Francis J. Fitzgerald, eds. Louisville, Kent.: AdCraft Sports Marketing, 1996. 56-59.

-----. "Horned Frogs Shock Ohio State, 18-14." *Greatest Moments in TCU Football History.* Dan Jenkins and Francis J. Fitzgerald, eds. Louisville, Kent.: AdCraft Sports Marketing, 1996. 146, 148- 49.

-----. "No. 1 TCU Tops Carnegie Tech." *Greatest Moments in TCU Football History.* Dan Jenkins and Francis J. Fitzgerald, eds. Louisville, Kent.: AdCraft Sports Marketing, 1996. 73-76.

-----. "Swink Stampedes for 4 Scores, Frogs Win, 47-20." *Greatest Moments in TCU Football History.* Dan Jenkins and Francis J. Fitzgerald, eds. Louisville, Kent.: AdCraft Sports Marketing, 1996. 128-32.

Heika, Mike. "Big 'D' at Dallas." *Greatest Moments in TCU Football History.* Dan Jenkins and Francis J. Fitzgerald, eds. Louisville, Kent.: AdCraft Sports Marketing, 1996. 209.

"In the Hunt." *The TCU Magazine.* Fall 1999. http://www.magarchive.tcu.edu/articles/1999-03-RR.asp?issueid=199903.

"Instant Classic: 'Rally Turtle Sends Frogs into Frenzy.'" *CollegeBaseball360.com.* 24 June 2010. http://collegebaseball360.com/2010/06/24/rattle-turtle-sends-frogs-into-frenzy.

Jones, Mike. "Razorbacks Frog-Tied." *Greatest Moments in TCU Football History.* Dan Jenkins and Francis J. Fitzgerald, eds. Louisville, Kent.: AdCraft Sports Marketing, 1996. 202-03.

-----. "Shocker: TCU 23, Texas 14." *Greatest Moments in TCU Football History.* Dan Jenkins and Francis J. Fitzgerald, eds. Louisville, Kent.: AdCraft Sports Marketing, 1996. 206-08.

-----. "TCU Stuns Arkansas, 32-31." *Greatest Moments in TCU Football History.* Dan Jenkins and Francis J. Fitzgerald, eds. Louisville, Kent.: AdCraft Sports Marketing, 1996. 185-87.

Kamen, Ed. "TCU Football: The Best of the Best -- Receiver." *KILLERFROGS.com.* 13 March 2012. http://www.killerfrogs.com/msgboard/index.php?showtopic=152338.

Kanyer, Wyatt. "Support and Recruiting Characterize Coach's Career." *tcu360.* 23 Nov. 2012. http://www.tcu360.com/mens-golf/2012/11/16522.

King, Clifford and Pat Truly. "Pittman's Death Mars Win." *Greatest Moments in TCU Football History.* Dan Jenkins and Francis J. Fitzgerald, eds. Louisville, Kent.: AdCraft Sports Marketing, 1996. 178-79.

Kix, Paul. "Alone No More." *Dallas Observer.* 31 March 2005. http://www.dallasobserver.com/2005-03-31/news/alone-no-more.

LeBreton, Gil. "Foreword." *Believe It! Rose Bowl Win Caps TCU's Perfect Season.* Chicago: Triumph Books, 2011. 6, 8.

-----. "Knowing All About Scary, TCU Feared Not Valley of Death." *Star-Telegram.com.* 27 Sept. 2009. http://nl.newsbank.com./nl-search/we/Archives?p_action=doc&p_docid=12B09CD0309F6E.

-----. "Patterson's Preparation Served Frogs Well in Boise." *Star-Telegram.com.* 14 Nov. 2011. http://nl.newsbank.com/nl-search/we/Archives?p_action=doc&p_docid=13C37E199A431.

-----. "TCU Wakes Up in Time to Smell the Poinsettia After Stinky Start." *Star-Telegram.com.* 22 Dec. 2011. http://nl.newsbank.com/nl-search/we/Archives?p_action=doc&p_docid=13BCBC6A5BAF.

-----. "TCU's Patterson Takes Victory in Stride." *Star-Telegram.com.* 23 Nov. 2012. http://nl.newsbank.com/nl-search/we/Archives?p_action=doc&p_docid=142BCECC06FC.

-----. "The Frogs Are Deserving Rose Bowl Champions." *Believe It! Rose Bowl Win Caps TCU's Perfect Season.* Chicago: Triumph Books, 2011. 20, 24, 26.

-----. "With Dislocated Elbow, TCU Shooter Shows Her Tough Side." *Star-Telegram.com.* 28 July 2012. http://www.star-telegram.com/2012/07/29/

4134408/with-dislocated-elbow-tcu-shooter.html.

MacArthur, John. *Twelve Ordinary Men*. Nashville: W Publishing Group, 2002.

Magill, Susie. "Coales of Wisdom." *Sharing the Victory*. March 2009. http://sharingthe
victory.com/vsItemDisplay.1sp?.

Mahan, Molly and Rick Waters. "The History of the Iron Skillet." *The TCU Magazine*. Fall
2009. http://www.magazine.tcu.edu/Magazine/Article.aspx?Articleid=199.

"Meet the Reaper -- Reggie Hunt." *GregorHutton.com*. http://www.gregorhutton.com/
reggiehunt/index3.html.

Montemer, Max. "Golfer Plans to Improve His Game in Japan After College." *tcu360*. 29
April 2013. http://www.tcu.360.com/mens-golf/2013/04/18011.

-----. "Trust, Experience Vital in Golf Coach's Recruiting Tactics." *tcu360*. 22 April 2013.
http://www.tcu360.com/mens-golf/2013/04/17932.

Moore, David. "TCU's Washington Finds the Magic." *Greatest Moments in TCU Football
History*. Dan Jenkins and Francis J. Fitzgerald, eds. Louisville, Kent.: AdCraft Sports
Marketing, 1996. 180-81.

Moore, Dick. "Meyer Built a Winner, But Missed the Roses." *Greatest Moments in TCU Football History*. Dan Jenkins and Francis J. Fitzgerald, eds. Louisville, Kent.:AdCraft
Sports Marketing, 1996. 126-27.

-----. "Punt Return by Thornton Ignites TCU." *Greatest Moments in TCU Football History*.
Dan Jenkins and Francis J. Fitzgerald, eds. Louisville, Kent.: AdCraft Sports
Marketing, 1996. 174-75.

Murphy, Austin. "Horned Frog Formula." *Sports Illustrated*. 12 Oct. 2009. http://sports
illustrated.cnn.com/vault/article/magazine/MAG1161009/index.htm.

Myers, Tracey. "Women's Insider: Dziuk a Pioneer for TCU Women." *Star-Telegram.com*.
7 Oct. 2002. http://nl.newsbank.com/nl-search/we/Archives?p_action=doc&p_
docid=0F689772E19A375.

"No. 4 TCU Crushes No. 16 Utah, 55-28: Frogs Avenge Last Season's Loss to Utes." *cstv.com*.
14 Nov. 2009. http://www.cstv.com/printable/schools/tcu/sports/m-footbl/recaps.

Paul, Johnny. "TCU Claims a Share of Title." *Greatest Moments in TCU Football History*. Dan
Jenkins and Francis J. Fitzgerald, eds. Louisville, Kent.: AdCraft Sports Marketing,
1996. 214-16.

Phillips, Troy. "The Old College Try." *The TCU Magazine*. Summer 2010. http://www.
magazine.tcu.edu/Magazine/Article.aspx?ArticleId=357.

Pierce, Damien. "Kicker Browne Is TCU's Point Man." *Star-Telegram.com*. 23 Oct. 2003.http://
nl-newsbank.com/nl-search/we/Archives?p_action=doc&p_docid=0FE7798F1FA3E.

Prater, Taylor. "Equestrian Horses Regarded as Teammates." *tcu360*. 8 April 2013. http://
www.tcu360.com/sports/2013.04/17760.

Riddle, Greg. "World-Class Speed." *The TCU Magazine*. Winter 2003. http://www.mag
archive.tcu.edu/article/2003-04-RR.asp?issueid=200304.

"Running to a Record: TCU's Tomlinson Breaks Single-Game Rushing Mark." *cnnsi.com*.
21 Nov. 1999. http://sportsillustrated.cnn.com/football/college/news/1999/11/20/
tomlinson_record.

"Sammy Baugh." *Wikipedia, the free encyclopedia*. http://en.wikipedia.org/wiki/Sammy_
Baugh.

Staples. Andy. "TCU's March Through Realignment Wilderness Finally Comes to End."
SI.com. 5 July 2012. http://sportsillustrated.cnn.com/2012/writers/andy_staples/
07/05/tcu-big-12-realignment.

Stevenson, Stefan. "A 35-3 Halftime Lead Shows How Big the Gap Is." *Believe It!: Rose Bowl
Win Caps TCU's Perfect Season*. Chicago: Triumph Books, 2011. 54, 56, 58.

-----. "As Expected, the No. 4-Ranked Horned Frogs Had Little Trouble." *Believe It!: Rose
Bowl Win Caps TCU's Perfect Season*. Chicago: Triumph Books, 2011. 42, 44, 46.

-----. "Assist on Verrett's Block Goes to Coach." *Star-Telegram.com*. 4 Nov. 2012. http://

nl.newsbank.com/nl-search/we/Archives?p_action=doc&p_docid=1426B47BB6A80.

-----. "For National Prestige, It's One Big Game for Frogs." *Star-Telegram.com*. 26 Sept. 2009. http://nl. newsbank.com/nl-search/we/Archives?p_action=doc&p_docid= 12AF9DF343C90E.

-----. "Frog Heaven: TCU Rocks Kansas in Stunning Upset." *Star-Telegram.com*. 7 Feb. 2013. http://nl.newsbank.com/nl-search/we/Archives?p_action=doc&p_docid= 1444DB6092A3A.

-----. "Frogs Rain on Clemson Parade." *Star-Telegram.com*. 27 Sept. 2009. http://nl.newsbank. com/nl-search/we/Archives?p_action=doc&p_docid=12B09CD0382492.

-----. "Frogs' Tight End Quickly Turns Into Starting Offensive Tackle." *Star-Telegram.com*. 1 Sept. 2011. http://nl.newsbank.com/nl-search/we/Archives?p_action=doc&p_ docid=1397CEE46297C.

-----. "Head of the Family Kenny Cain Draws on Toughness, Team Bonds to Lead Young TCU Defense." *Star-Telegram.com*. 29 Sept. 2012. http://nl.newsbank.com/nl-search/ we/Archives?p_action=doc&p_docid=141B2A831FBF7.

-----. "Second-Half Turnaround Sparked TCU Against Louisiana Tech." *Star-Telegram.com*. 23 Dec. 2011. http://nl.newsbank.com/nl-search/we/Archives?p_action=doc&p_ docid=13BD10F2079888.

-----. "Tank Driven to Succeed: Accident at 13 Gave Carder Determination to Make Big Things Happen." *Star-Telegram.com*. 24 Oct. 2009. http://nl.newsbank.com/nl-search/ we/Archives?p_action=doc&p_docid=12B9D6BCF884A.

-----. "TCU Crushes Flyers to Stay Alive." *Star-Telegram.com*. 3 June 2012. http://nl. newsbank.com/nl-search/we/Archives?p_action=doc&p_docid=13F695EE9B338.

-----. "TCU Finishes Perfect Season with Rose Bowl Win." *Believe It!: Rose Bowl Win Caps TCU's Perfect Season*. Chicago: Triumph Books, 2011.10, 14, 16.

-----. "TCU Recovers from 11-Run Meltdown to Scrape Win in Ninth." *Star-Telegram.com*. 25 May 2012. htttp://nl.newsbank.com/nl-search/we/Archives?p_action=doc&p_ docid=13EFCF0629BB2.

-----. "TCU Senior Deck Finds New Home at Right Tackle." *Star-Telegram.com*. 19 Oct. 2011. http://nl.newsbank.com/nl-search/we/Archives?p_action=doc&p_docid= 13A7A0E74B54.

-----. "TCU's Upset of Kansas Feels Like a Distant Memory as Teams Meet for Rematch." *Star-Telegram.com*. 22 Feb. 2013. http://nl.newsbank.com/nl-search/we/Arvhices?p_ action=doc&p_docid=1449F7192BDF8.

-----. "Thank You, Lee Corso." *Believe It!: Rose Bowl Win Caps TCU's Perfect Season*. Chicago: Triumph Books, 2011. 36, 38, 40.

-----. "The Defense Shines, But Offense Takes a While." *Believe It!: Rose Bowl Win Caps TCU's Perfect Season*. Chicago: Triumph Books, 2011. 66, 68, 70.

-----. "Thomas Scores 32 as TCU Stages Stunner to Beat No. 11 UNLV." *Star-Telegram.com*. 15 Feb. 2012. http://nl.newsbank.com/nl-search/we/Archives?p_action=doc&p_ docid=13DF7E969D4A.

-----. "Wake-Up Call: TCU Coach Irked at Frogs' Missteps After Miracle at Daniel-Meyer." *Star-Telegram.com*. 8 Feb. 2013. http://nl.newsbank.com/nl-search/we/Archives?p_ action=doc&p_docid=14452FA9E64516.

-----. "Williamson Not Afraid: TCU Coach Living Life to the Fullest." *Believe It!: Rose Bowl Win Caps TCU's Perfect Season*. Chicago: Triumph Books, 2011. 116, 118-19.

"Tank Carder." *Wikipedia, the free encyclopedia*. en.wikipedia.org/wiki/Tank_Carder.

"TCU 28, USC 19." *SI.com*. 31 Dec. 1998. http://sportsillustrated.cnn.com/football/college/ scoreboards/1998/12/31/recap.tcu.usc.html.

"TCU Denies Wisconsin on Late 2-Point Try to Win Rose Bowl." *ESPN.com*. 1 Jan. 2011. http://scores.espn.go.com/ncf/recap?gameId=310012628.

"TCU's New Horned Frog Is the Apex of Intimidation." *bigleadsports*. 24 March 2013. http://www.thebiglead.com/index.php/2013/03/24/tcus-new-horned-frog-is-the-apex-of-intimidation.

Tiongson, Beau. "Former Frog Finds Spot on Depth Chart in Italy." *tcu360.com*. 29 April 2013. http://www.*tcu360.com*/football/2013/04/18013.

"TKO'd by TCU." *SI.com*. 3 Sept. 2005. http://sportsillustrated.cnn.com/vault/article/web/COM1038880/index/index.htm.

Ubben, David. "Purke Stymies Seminoles in CWS Opener." *ESPN.com*. 19 June 2010. http://espn.go.com/ncaa/blog/_/name/ncaa_baseball/id/5306296.

Underwood, John. "A Big Ol' Country Boy With a Big Ol' Country Pass." *Sports Illustrated*. 15 Oct. 1962. http://sportsillustrated.cnn.com/vault/article/magazine/MAG1074203/index.htm.

Waters, John. "College Football." *Sports Illustrated*. 26 Sept. 1994. http://sportsillustrated.cnn.com/vault/article/magazine/MAG1005729/index.htm.

Waters, Rick. "Another Off-the-Bench Hero." *The TCU Magazine*. Winter 2005. http://www.magarchive.tcu.edu/articles/2005-04-rr.asp?issueid=200504.

-----. "At Home on the Court." *The TCU Magazine*. Fall 2007. http://www.magarchive.tcu/edu/articles/2007-04-RR6.asp.

-----. "Borrowed Brilliance." *The TCU Magazine*. Winter 2008. http://www.magarchive.tcu.edu/articles/2008-03-RR3.asp.

-----. "From Kicked Out to Kick-Started." *The TCU Magazine*. Fall 2010. http://www.magazine.tcu.edu/Magazine/Article.aspx?ArticleId=414.

-----. "Getting His Kicks." *The TCU Magazine*. Winter 2007. http://www.magarchive.tcu.edu/articles/2007-04-RRf.asp.

-----. "Inspired by Family." *The TCU Magazine*. Winter 2009. http://www.mgazine.tcu.edu/Magazine/Article.aspx?ArticleId=260.

-----. "Making His Own Legend." *The TCU Magazine*. Fall 2012. http://www.magazine.tcu.edu.Magazine/Article.aspx?ArticleId=713.

-----. "Redemption in the Crosshairs." *The TCU Magazine*. Spring 2006. http://www.magarchive.tcu/edu/articles/2006-02-RR6.asp.

-----. "Success Comes in Threes." *The TCU Magazine*. Winter 2006. http://www.magarchive.tcu/edu/articles/2006-01-rr4.asp.

Welch, Morgan. "Equestrian: Being Prepared for the Unexpected." *tcu360*. 5 Dec. 2012. http://www.tcu360.com/sports/2012/12/16637.

Wilkins, Galen. "Butterflies Aside, Freshman Frog Turns in Exceptional Game." *Greatest Moments in TCU Football History*. Dan Jenkins and Francis J. Fitzgerald, eds. Louisville, Kent.: AdCraft Sports Marketing, 1996. 200-01.

Williams, Charean. "'Your Reason to Believe': Former TCU Standout Refusing to Let Cancer Delay NFL Career." *Star-Telegram.com*. 3 July 2011. http://nl.newsbank.com/nl-search/we/Archives?p_action=doc&p_docid=13840867ABBD.

Wright, Mark. "Back in Business." *The TCU Magazine*. Spring 2008. http://www.magarchive.tcu/edu/articles/2008-01-RR4.asp.

Wulffsen, Don L. "Unconscious Player Preserves TCU Victory." *Greatest Moments in TCU Football History*. Dan Jenkins and Francis J. Fitzgerald, eds. Louisville, Kent.: AdCraft Sports Marketing, 1996. 72.

Yarina, Brent. "Former Soccer Player Emerges as Strong Kicker." *TCU Daily Skiff*. 29 Aug. 2003. http://www.skiff.tcu.edu/fall2003/082903/form.html.

HORNED FROGS

INDEX
(LAST NAME, DEVOTION DAY NUMBER)

204